MY YEARS ON THE STAGE

From a portrait by Joseph De Camp in the collection of The Players.

JOHN DREW

MY YEARS ON THE STAGE

BY
JOHN DREW

WITH A FOREWORD BY
BOOTH TARKINGTON

NEW YORK
E. P. DUTTON & COMPANY
681 FIFTH AVENUE

FOREWORD

How long ago is it, old schoolmate, since two "middlers" from Exeter rollicked down to New York for an Easter vacation, and on an imperishable evening glamoured their young memories permanently with Augustin Daly's company of players at Daly's Theatre and *The Taming of the Shrew?*

What a good and merry town was brown-stone New York then, when one stood at the doors of the Fifth Avenue Hotel to see the pretty girls from all over the country parading by after the matinee; when the Avenue was given over to proud horses and graceful women; when there were no automobiles and only a few telephones; when Ada Rehan was playing *Katherine* at Daly's and when those two Exeter school-boys got the impression that the whole place belonged, in a general way, to the *Petruchio* who tamed her, John Drew!

The earth must have swung round the sun a few times since then, my schoolmate, for now comes that gay young *Petruchio* before us with his Memoirs! He

v

feels that he has memories to entertain and to enlighten us; he has now lived long enough to have seen something of the stage and of the world, it appears. For one, I am willing to read him. I have listened to him so often since that ancient night at Daly's; and though the words I've heard him say were words suggested by some paltry fellow of a playwright, yet I've had such entertainment of the man, so much humor and delight, I am even eager to hear him, now that he will speak in his own words of himself and of his life, his art and his friends. As to this last, though, he will have to select with care; he could never tell us much of all his friends, were Methuselah from birth to grave his diligent amanuensis.

What he has played most congenially, and with the manliest humor of his time, have been the rôles of gentlemen; and there is a certain thing about his book of which we are already sure before we read it: therein he cannot fail to add one more to the long, fine gallery of portraits of gentlemen he has shown us; and this one must necessarily be the best gentleman of them all. And it will be the one we have liked best, ever discerning it behind the others; for it was always there, and turned many a playwright's shoddy outline into a fine fellow. John Drew would play *Simon Legree* into a misunderstood gentleman, I believe.

The reason is a simple one: he was born with a taste for the better side of things and the cleaner surfaces of life. He has found them more interesting and more congenial than mire, and if he should ever deal with mire he would deal with it cleanly. Here was the nature of the man always present in his acting; and I think it has been because of that and because of his humor—his own distinctive humor—that he has charmed the best American public throughout so many fortunate years. John Drew has been an actual feature of the best American life ever since his youth—indeed, he is one of its institutions; and there is a long gratitude due him. His Memoirs may properly be greeted, in fact, as we should greet a birthday speech at the banquet we are too numerous to make for him; that is, with cheers as he rises to address us. And then as we settle down to listen we may be sure we shall hear of many an old-time familiar figure besides himself, for John Drew has known "pretty much everybody" of his generation. His generation still continues, it is pleasant and reassuring to know; for he admits us to the intimacy of this autographical mood of his long

before the fireside years claim him. And he may speak
to us freely, with as good assurance as he has always
had, that whenever he speaks at all it is "among
friends."

BOOTH TARKINGTON

Kennebunkport, Maine.
July, 1921.

ILLUSTRATIONS

MY YEARS ON THE STAGE

we would like to hope that her daughter and son are also representatives of it. Miss Drew has appeared but two or three times upon the stage, and the impression she then created was favorable. Her worst faults are her youth and inexperience, and both these time will overcome. Of Mr. Drew we know nothing. But remembering with profound gratitude the pleasure that the mother and father of these children have given the public, how great and conscientious an artist Mrs. Drew is, and John Drew was, we trust for their sakes that the old playgoers of Philadelphia will unite on Saturday to give the young players, just entering upon the career by which they are to live, a substantial, hearty welcome. It may be that for their own sakes they deserve such welcome; but whether this be so or not they deserve it for the sake of those great artists whose children they are, and who for so many years gave of their best to the pleasure and entertainment of the town.

We know of no opportunity so favorable for the public to show its respect for the memory of the great dead comedian, or gratitude to his wife, who survives him, as that which will be presented on Saturday night.

The first lines that I spoke on any stage give an idea of the self-possession of the character of *Plumper* that I played in *Cool as a Cucumber*, even if they do not indicate my own self-possession and confidence. I was ushered on by a maid, a part played on that night by my mother. I addressed her: "My name, did you

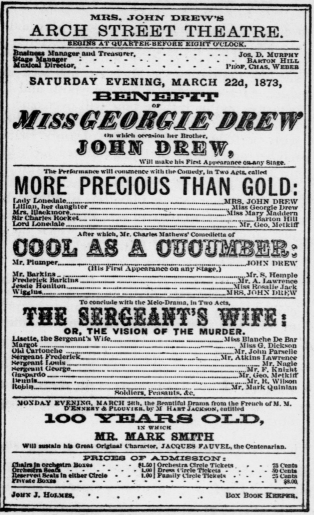

MRS. JOHN DREW'S
ARCH STREET THEATRE.
BEGINS AT QUARTER-BEFORE EIGHT O'CLOCK.

Business Manager and Treasurer, ... JOS. D. MURPHY
Stage Manager . . . . BARTON HILL
Musical Director, ... PROF. CHAS. WEBER

SATURDAY EVENING, MARCH 22d, 1873,
BENEFIT
OF
Miss GEORGIE DREW
On which occasion her Brother,
JOHN DREW,
Will make his First Appearance on any Stage.

The Performance will commence with the Comedy, in Two Acts, called
MORE PRECIOUS THAN GOLD:
Lady Lonedale...MRS. JOHN DREW
Lillian, her daughter ....Miss Georgie Drew
Mrs. Blackmore...Miss Mary Maddern
Sir Charles Rocket..Barton Hill
Lord Lonedale ....Mr. Geo. Metkiff

After which, Mr. Charles Mathews' Comedietta of
COOL AS A CUCUMBER:
Mr. Plumper..JOHN DREW
(His First Appearance on any Stage.)
Mr. Barkins ....Mr. S. Hemple
Frederick Barkins ....Mr. A. Lawrence
Jessie Houlton ....Miss Rosalie Jack
Wiggins...MRS. JOHN DREW

To conclude with the Melo-Drama, in Two Acts,
THE SERGEANT'S WIFE:
OR, THE VISION OF THE MURDER.
Lisette, the Sergeant's Wife...................................Miss Blanche De Bar
Margot ....Miss G. Dickson
Old Cartouche ....Mr. John Parselle
Sergeant Frederick ....Mr. Atkins Lawrence
Sergeant Louis ....Mr. Nagle
Sergeant George..Mr. F. Knight
Gaspardo ....Mr. Geo. Metkiff
Dennis...Mr. R. Wilson
Robin..Mr. Mark Quinlan
Soldiers, Peasants, &c.

MONDAY EVENING, MARCH 24th, the Beautiful Drama from the French of M. M.
D'ENNERY & PLOUVIER, by M. HART JACKSON, entitled
100 YEARS OLD,
IN WHICH
MR. MARK SMITH
Will sustain his Great Original Character, JACQUES FAUVEL, the Centenarian.

PRICES OF ADMISSION:
Chairs in Orchestra Boxes . . . . $1.50 | Orchestra Circle Tickets . . . . 75 Cents
Orchestra Seats . . . . 1.00 | Dress Circle Tickets . . . . 50 Cents
Reserved Seats in either Circle . . 1.00 | Family Circle Tickets . . . . 25 Cents
Private Boxes $8.00

JOHN J. HOLMES, ... BOX BOOK KEEPER.

From Theatre Collection, Harvard University.

MR. PLUMPER   JOHN DREW
(First appearance on any stage)

3

Evening Bulletin: "Considering the circumstances, his self-possession was remarkable."

Of course I had known the theatre almost from infancy. Early among my recollections are conversations between my mother and my grandmother about changed conditions in the theatre, and that what was going on then at the Arch Street Theatre in Philadelphia and Wallack's in New York was very different from the old days. These conversations between the two actresses would always end with some such discussion as to whether it was the spring of '29 or '30 that they had played in Natchez, Vicksburg and other places in the South.

This Southern tour seems to have been made in the spring of 1829, for I have a volume of Shakespeare's plays in which is written on the fly leaf: "This volume, comprising the entire works of the immortal dramatist, is presented to Miss Louisa Lane as a feeble, though an appropriate and sincere testimony of her extraordinary genius and intellectual worth by C. Griffin, of Natchez, March, 1829."

At the time that inscription was written my mother, Louisa Lane, was nine years old. The act, *Twelve Precisely*, which she played so successfully, seems to have been a protean sketch or skit in which she assumed five characters. There is a lithograph published

THE MOTHER AND FATHER OF JOHN DREW

THE EARLIEST PICTURE OF JOHN DREW

in Boston in 1828, which depicts Miss Lane, eight
years of age, in the five characters in *Twelve Precisely*.
Of this performance at the old Chestnut Street Theatre in Philadelphia one of the newspapers said:

> This astonishing little creature evinces a talent
> for and a knowledge of the stage beyond what
> we find in many experienced performers of merit.
> The entertainment of *Twelve Precisely* is well
> adapted to the display of the versatility of her
> powers; and in the *Irish Girl* she may, with truth,
> be pronounced inimitably comic. Her brogue and
> manner are excellent. The *Young Soldier* was
> also admirably assumed.

In February, 1828, Louisa Lane appeared as *Albert*
to Edwin Forrest's *William Tell*. The latter seems
to have been so pleased that he presented my mother
with a silver medal on which is inscribed: "Presented
by E. Forrest to Miss L. Lane as a testimonial of his
admiration for her talents."

CHAPTER TWO

I WAS born in 1853, and my birthday was November 13—the same day as Edwin Booth's. I was christened January 10, 1854, in St. Stephen's Church. This was my mother's birthday. My godfathers were William Wheatley, who was associated with my father in the management of the Arch Street Theatre, and William Sheridan, who as William S. Fredericks was the stage manager of the same theatre. My godmother was Mrs. D. P. Bowers, one of the best known actresses on the American stage and a great friend of my mother's. She played *Lady Audley*, *East Lynne* and *Camille* through the country with great success. I was born at 269 (according to the new numbering 709) South Tenth Street, Philadelphia. Later we moved to Buttonwood Street, and when my mother took over the management of the Arch Street Theatre, which had earlier been managed by my father and William Wheatley, we lived first on Eighth Street and then on Ninth, so that my mother might be near the theatre which was at Sixth and Arch.

I vaguely remember the Buttonwood Street house

and I know that it was to this house that my father, a successful portrayer of Irish comedy rôles, came back from one of his several trips to Ireland, bringing with him an Irish donkey that was allowed to roam for a short time in our back yard and was then sold. This donkey seemed to me to be a huge steed and is, I think, my earliest recollection.

I cannot remember a time when I was not interested in games. Riding was always my favorite sport. At a tender age I was sent to Madame Minna's Riding Academy. I had only had one or two lessons when I was thrown, and the horse stepped on the crown of my hat. Before I had time to be frightened the riding master put me back in the saddle, cramped my leg down and said: "You're all right now." I think this kept me from losing my nerve.

I do not remember when I learned to swim, nor do I remember a time at which I did not row. I rowed on the Schuylkill River and belonged to the Malta Boat Club, of which I am still an honorary member. The boys in my day played baseball, and, of course, we played cricket, being Philadelphians. I was very fond of fencing and took it up long before I decided to go on the stage. In the Arch Street Theatre there was a large space back of the balcony where we held fencing classes. In my early years in the theatre fencing was a very necessary part of the actor's equipment, for it was supposed to lend grace to the carriage as well as being necessary in so many of the plays. In later years I won a fencing championship of the New York Athletic Club.

It is the house at 119 North Ninth Street that I associate with my boyhood. It was a conventional Philadelphia house, with white shutters and white steps. We were not in an exceptional or fashionable neighborhood. A great many of our neighbors were Quakers. My chief playmate was Isaac T. Hopper, named for his grandfather, the great abolitionist. Next to us in Buttonwood Street had lived the Quaker, Passmore Williamson, who was much interested in the underground railroad by which slaves were escaping to Canada.

Passmore Williamson figured in a sensational case in the late fifties. Colonel John H. Wheeler, the United States minister to Nicaragua, was on a steamboat at one of the Delaware wharves. Three slaves belonging to him were sitting at his side on the upper deck. Just as the signal bell was ringing Passmore Williamson went up to the slaves and told them that they were free. The slaves did not wish to leave their master but a negro mob took them ashore. The legal action and arguments resulting from this consumed

From Theatre Collection, Harvard University.

A DAGUERROTYPE OF MRS. JOHN DREW, SENIOR, AS
OPHELIA

much time and filled a volume. During part of the
time Williamson was defended by Edward Hopper,
the father of my playmate.

Young Hopper's mother was a daughter of Lucretia
Mott. I remember so well that wonderful woman, and
how much she impressed me even then. With my playmate I used to visit her country place, which in those
days seemed so far out of town. It was at City Line,
and the Mott place was called Roadside. First there
was a long ride in a horse car to the North Pennsylvania train. Here on one occasion I saw Lord and
Lady Amberly, who were interested in abolition and
the reforms to which Lucretia Mott devoted so much
time and attention. While I do not recall now any
of the conversations, I remember that it was very different from what I heard at home and most of these
people talked what the Quakers called the "common
language."

I was taken to hear Wendell Phillips by the Hoppers and the Motts. I was impressed because they were
but I was really too young.

One day I came back from Roadside and told my
mother and grandmother that I had seen women sew-
ing on Sunday. In our own household the toys and
books of my sisters and myself were put away on Sunday. My grandmother was somewhat surprised that

people would sew on Sunday. Her own idea of Sunday occupation was *the Spirit of Missions*, which she read literally from cover to cover. My grandmother, Mrs. Kinloch, had played in a number of theatrical companies in this country and England, and had been forced to withdraw from a company in New Orleans because she refused to act on Sunday. Sunday performances were then as now the custom in New Orleans. As a very young boy I can remember going to St. Stephen's with my grandmother, who gave the responses in a very loud voice which seemed to me the height of religious fervor.

Before I was ten I went to a school at a place called Village Green, which was made a military school while I was there. I hated to leave home, but going away got me out of one difficulty. I had the greatest trouble with my speech. I talked with that same accent or intonation that Philadelphians, no matter of what degree, always seem to have.

I can remember the extreme annoyance of my grandmother. She would protest to my mother: "Louisa, I cannot understand a word the boy says."

I would try and pronounce words as they told me to at home. It was no use, and while I probably improved somewhat under the instruction of these two actresses, who had been trained in the old school of elocution, I was glad to escape to the street and my playmates.

I spent my tenth birthday at Village Green. I have a letter from my mother dated "Philadelphia, November 12, 1863":

> My dear Son: I received yours of the ninth inst. today. Tomorrow will be your birthday, my darling—you are ten years old tomorrow. All your family wish you many, many happy returns of the day. I can't send you any birthday present, as you are soon to come home. Sorry that the shoes are too large, but if you can get along till you come home, I will get you a pair to fit better. Of course you can take your sledge back with you. Take good care of yourself, and as it is cold early in the morning, don't waste time in dressing yourself.
>
> All send love. God bless you dear.
>
> Your affectionate mother,
>
> LOUISA DREW.

From Village Green I went to another boarding school at Andalusia in Bucks County, Pennsylvania. Here four of us had a room together, and we had to get up in turn and make the fire in a Franklin stove. I was very young, the youngest boy in the school, and particularly poor at fire making. When my turn came I received jibes and advice from my three schoolmates in their luxurious and warm beds.

This school was a sectarian one, and a place with some reputation in Philadelphia; but a friend of the family, who had boys in the school, thought it did not give a good education in the classics, and so I was taken out of boarding school and sent to the Episcopal Academy in Philadelphia. I do not suppose that I was a very good student. The things I liked, Latin and French, I kept up for years afterward. In arithmetic I was shocking. Together with the other boys of the day, I regarded my teachers as natural enemies. Most of the schoolboys were in some cadet corps. The older boys were drilling, because they thought they might be called to the colors in a year or two. I was the youngest boy in the corps commanded by one Major Eckendorf; and there is a picture of me in uniform, taken at Germon's Photograph Gallery, on Chestnut Street, which has always been called in the family "The Hero of Gettysburg." This was taken in July, 1863, just after the battle of Gettysburg.

My first recollection of an officer was not Major Eckendorf, but my uncle, Edward Drew. On his way to the front he came through Philadelphia and stopped at our house. He was a captain in Berdan's sharpshooters. He wore one of those Civil War uniforms with long, blue frock-coat effect, single-breasted, with brass buttons. He had long side whiskers called Pic-

"THE HERO OF GETTYSBURG"

This photograph of John Drew was taken in July, 1863, just after the battle.

cadilly weepers, which gave him a sort of *Dundreary* appearance. He showed my father an entirely new sighting device which was then being distributed to his men.

School was much interrupted in Civil War days, and my companions who had fathers, older brothers or relatives in the war would disappear for a day or two and then come back somewhat subdued and with some evidence of mourning.

In a thoughtless way I felt somewhat out of things. One morning I came down to breakfast to find my mother and my grandmother in tears. My mother was reading aloud a letter telling of the death of my uncle, Edward Drew. He had been killed in action.

I hurried to school to declare myself in the "movement" because I, too, had lost some one. My uncle had seemed to me very smart with his brass buttons and wonderful whiskers, but the satisfaction of being in the "game" with my companions outweighed the loss of an uncle that I really did not know. Still, the fact that he was killed in action affected me more than the death of my uncle, George Drew, who had been sent back to Buffalo, where he died of wounds.

The fall of Richmond meant to us a half-holiday; and then one morning on my way to school I heard that Lincoln had been shot. I rushed back to the house to

CHAPTER THREE

IN these late years, when I have been playing Philadelphia, I have made pilgrimages to the different places that were associated with my youth.

My old school is one of them, the Episcopal Academy at Juniper and Locust Streets; the school has moved out into the country towards Haverford, but the building still stands.

I walk to Logan Square, where I attended a fair with my mother in the early days of the Civil War. It was called a Sanitary Fair, because it was held under the auspices of the Sanitary Commission. I have an album that my mother bought me there.

I go to St. Stephen's Church, Tenth Street near Chestnut, now in a kind of sordid neighborhood. The church was rehabilitated a comparatively short time ago. The last time I was there I asked to see the baptismal register and found out that I was christened on my mother's birthday, January 10, 1854.

There was a young woman doing some work in the church and, after I pointed out the entry on the register, she said: "Oh, I have something that may interest you."

She brought out a box containing a great many odds and ends, and from it took a silver plate. It brought back memories of going to Sunday School and then being taken into church afterward and being dismissed by my grandmother, Mrs. Kinloch, before the sermon. That silver plate had been on my mother's pew in St. Stephen's for more than sixty years. On the plate was engraved "L. Drew."

I walk down and look at the front of the Arch Street Theatre, which holds so many memories. It has fallen on different days and has been in turn a German, a variety, a Yiddish theatre.

My mother took over the lease of the Arch Street Theatre in 1861, and the first play that I remember anything at all about is one called *Scotto, the Scout*, an ephemeral thing that was a concession to the great interest in the war. I do not know whether or not this was the first play that I saw nor do I know who wrote it. I imagine that it was hastily fashioned from stock material with a little added war interest. So far as I know it was never done in any other theatre. To the usual stock characters of the day was added the then prominent *General MacDowell* and a number of negroes.

My father also appeared in *Handy Andy*, *Knight of Arva*, or *Connor the Rash*, the *Irish Emigrant* and Samuel Lover's *Rory O'More*, all successful and popular plays of the day. He did play other parts, and in the Tallis edition of Shakespeare there is a picture of him as *Sir Andrew* in *Twelfth Night*—a part I was to play many years later in support of Adelaide Neilson. But it was in the Irish rôles that he made his great success. He went to California by way of the Isthmus, and from there he went to Australia and then to London and Ireland. I have a letter from him, dated "Melbourne, Victoria, October 17, 1859." It begins:

> I went the other day to buy a book for your dear little sister Louisa and among others I found this. I have cut these leaves out and send them to you because they speak of a little boy named John Drew.

This is written on the back of the illustrated rhymes which begin:

> Who would have believed it,
>   If it were not proved true,
> That so pretty a lad
>   As was little John Drew,
> The pet of his sisters,
>   The hope of his dad,
> Should have such an objection
>   To washing and dressing—

These verses go on to show how the youthful hero of this sad tale degenerated until his clothes looked like a coal sack:

> His playmates forsook him,
>   What else could they do?
> And at length a man took him,
>   What else could they do?
> —Alas! Johnny Drew—
> Upon soot bags, to sleep,
>   In a cellar so deep,
> And bound him apprentice,
>   To work as a sweep.

Upon his world tour my father was accompanied by my elder sister and my aunt. He came back to Philadelphia early in 1862, played an engagement of several months in his repertoire at the Arch Street Theatre, and in May of that year he died.

The Freeman's Journal, of Dublin, printed the fact of his death with black rules or borders around the column. He was very popular there and highly regarded as an exponent of the Irish drama, which in those days was romantic comedy and nothing like the Harrigan and Hart Irish plays done in New York at a later period; nor were they at all similar to the Irish Theatre of Lady Gregory and Synge.

I saw a number of early performances that impressed me greatly. Three of these were by the greatest actors of the day. At the Walnut Street Theatre I saw Edwin Forrest in *Richelieu*, and Edwin Booth in Tom Taylor's play, *The Fool's Revenge*, at the Chestnut Street Theatre, and E. L. Davenport as *Sir Giles Overreach* in Massinger's play, *A New Way to Pay Old Debts*. I also saw such popular performances as that of Joseph Proctor in *Nick of the Woods*. And then there was that fine actor William E. Sheridan in a number of plays with the Chestnut Street Theatre Stock company but I do not believe that I saw him in any important rôle. Sheridan left the stage to enlist and rose to be a captain. He was wounded several times and one of his wounds disabled his hand.

Our house in Ninth Street was visited by these men when they were playing in Philadelphia, and Sunday night there was almost always some one connected with the theatre for supper. My mother had played in so many companies and had been in the theatre so long that the Booths, the Jeffersons and many others were intimately associated with the family.

I saw both the Prince of Wales and Charles Dickens in the "sixties." My grandmother took me to see the former. He appeared on the balcony of the old Continental Hotel, looking not unlike the present Prince of Wales on his recent visit. There was nothing to suggest the rather heavy, bearded man who, in the summer of 1888, sent for Ada Rehan and myself to come to his box in the Gaiety Theatre, London, during a performance of *The Taming of the Shrew*.

I heard Charles Dickens give a reading from "Pickwick Papers" on his second American tour. So great was the crowd that we were shown to our seats through the stage entrance. My mother, grandmother, sisters and Robert Craig, a young comedian in my mother's company, went to hear the great novelist.

As I remember, the reading was in the old Concert Hall in Chestnut Street where, with the Motts and the Hoppers, I had heard Wendell Phillips.

Craig was late by reason of rehearsing, but he arrived at the reading in time to get what he wanted of the Dickens mannerisms and intonation and appearance. Craig had marvelous powers as a mimic, and he was particularly good in his imitation of the novelist. Nothing he did in the Arch Street Theatre was quite so popular as the skits he wrote and in which he appeared as Dickens.

Upon the invitation of my mother Charles Dickens visited the Arch Street Theatre and saw a performance of *Ours*. This piece of Tom Robertson's was always in the repertoire, just as it was at Wallack's, and was a great favorite of my mother's. In asking Dickens to come to the theatre my mother assured him that his visit would not be made known in advance, and that he need not fear that he would be annoyed by curious crowds. He wrote her a very gracious and charming letter thanking her.

As there were no touring companies in those days, plays were usually sold for the different towns. My mother had an arrangement with Lester Wallack, by which she had the first choice of all the plays that he bought from the English authors. When she considered doing one of these, she would go to New York to see the Wallack production and judge it not only for Philadelphia audiences but with an idea as to its suitability for the Arch Street Theatre company.

It was on one of these trips to look over a play that I first saw New York, that is the New York of theatres, hotels and restaurants. Before this I had been brought over to see the *Great Eastern* on its arrival after its first voyage by John Sefton, an old friend of the family. The boat was somewhere in the North River as I remember. We left Philadelphia early in the morning and went back that same night. John Sefton, who accompanied me, had been years in the theatre and in the days before the railroads, when it was necessary to cross the mountains in a coach, he had been a member of a stock company in Pittsburg.

When I visited New York with my mother we

stopped at The Irving House, which was at Broadway and Twelfth Street, and dined at Delmonico's, that celebrated shrine of epicures, then at Fifth Avenue and Fourteenth Street. William Winter, who was then and for so many years after, a dramatic critic, came up and talked to my mother. Later, at Daly's Theatre, I came to know him very well. We then went to Wallack's to see *Lost in London*. Wallack's was at Broadway and Thirteenth Street, and the Rialto had had not moved so far north as Union Square, nor had Palmer's Theatre in Union Square been built.

In *Lost in London* Madelaine Henriques was the leading woman. She was one of the first women on the American stage to acquire a reputation for dressing parts well. The part of *Gilbert Featherstone* was played by Charles Fisher, who was a member of Augustin Daly's company when I joined it; and Charles Rockwell and I, the two youngest members of the Daly company, were ushers at his wedding many years afterward.

My mother's company at the Arch Street Theatre was considered a very good one and ranked with Wallack's in New York. The company remained from year to year much the same. I remember a few of the players: Robert Craig was first comedian, and Lizzie Price, who married that famous actor, Charles Fechter,

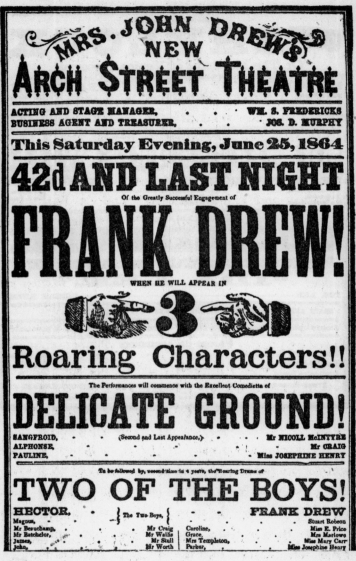

MRS. JOHN DREW'S
NEW
ARCH STREET THEATRE

ACTING AND STAGE MANAGER, · · · WM. S. FREDERICKS
BUSINESS AGENT AND TREASURER, · · JOS. D. MURPHY

This Saturday Evening, June 25, 1864

42d AND LAST NIGHT

Of the Greatly Successful Engagement of

FRANK DREW!

WHEN HE WILL APPEAR IN

3

Roaring Characters!!

The Performances will commence with the Excellent Comedietta of

DELICATE GROUND!

SANGFROID, · (Second and Last Appearance,) · · Mr NICOLL McINTYRE
ALPHONSE, · · · · · Mr CRAIG
PAULINE, · · · · · Miss JOSEPHINE HENRY

To be followed by, second time in 4 years, the Roaring Drama of

TWO OF THE BOYS!

HECTOR, · · { The Two Boys, } · · FRANK DREW

Magnus,				Stuart Robson
Mr Beauchamp,		Mr Craig	Caroline,	Miss E. Price
Mr Batchelor,		Mr Wallis	Grace,	Mrs Marlowe
James,		Mr Stull	Mrs Templeton,	Miss Mary Carr
John,		Mr Worth	Parker,	Miss Josephine Henry

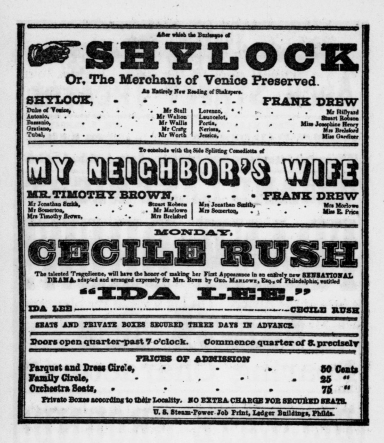

PLAYBILL, ARCH STREET THEATRE, PHILADELPHIA, 1864

31

CHAPTER FOUR

WHEN my mother took over the management of the Arch Street Theatre, it was all renovated and was in pretty fair condition for the time, but it had been built in 1827 and had an unmistakable theatre smell that was unlike anything else. I do not know whether this came from the gas fumes or the combination of the gas fumes and the new paint on the scenery, for there was always fresh paint in the theatre in spite of the fact that the scenery was not elaborate in the sense of today. A good deal of it was "flats" which were pushed on from both sides and met in the center. One half might be a cottage and the other a green wood.

Occasionally there was a play that was called "a production," and required, because of its elaborateness, a good many extra rehearsals. One such, called *Surf*, by Olive Logan, I remember distinctly. The scene was at Cape May, then a fashionable place for Philadelphians to go. Breakers were made by white cotton cloth and barrels. Just how it was arranged I do

OHN DREW BEFORE HE WENT ON
THE STAGE

JOHN DREW AT THE TIME OF
HIS FIRST APPEARANCE

ADA REHAN WHEN SHE APPEARED
WITH THE ARCH STREET THE-
ATRE COMPANY

not know, but in spite of the fact that the play was rather indifferent, it had a run of eight weeks, which at that time was considered a long run. Augustin Daly bought the rights for New York, where he produced it with some share of success.

A day in the Arch Street Theatre started with a rehearsal which began at ten o'clock in the morning and lasted about four hours. Sometimes when the bill was changing frequently there was more than one play to rehearse. The afternoon we usually had to ourselves for study. The performance began at eight, and Saturdays were our only matinee days.

The season after I went on the stage a new young woman was introduced to the company. She came to the theatre with her sister, whose stage name was Hattie O'Neill. Their eldest sister, Mrs. Oliver Doud Byron, had written to my mother that she wanted her sisters to play in the Arch Street Theatre. From Mrs. Byron's letter my mother got the impression that the name of the younger sister was Ada C. Rehan and, thinking that a middle initial was of no help to an actress, she had the name put in the bill as Ada Rehan, although actually the name was Ada Crehan. Ada made a hit, and so by this accident of my mother's there was named for all time in the theatre an actress who was to be the *Katherine* when I was *Petruchio* in the

overture I lured the prompter from his place and then blew through the tube as the leader answered the signal. A very pale and much whitened orchestra leader received a great laugh from his men and the people sitting down front.

As three or four other young people in the company were accused in turn, I had to own up. The calling down that I got from an infuriated manager-mother had better be left to the imagination.

That same season Frank Chanfrau came to Philadelphia to play his celebrated character of *Kit* in *The Arkansas Traveler*, supported by the Arch Street Theatre Company. Ada Rehan, her sister, Hattie O'Neill, Georgie and I all played in this piece. Chanfrau was related by marriage to Alexina Fisher Baker. Mrs. Baker was a great friend of my mother's and had also been something of an infant prodigy or, as Dickens' *Mr. Vincent Crummles* would say, an "infant phenomenon." My sisters and I had known the Baker children, Josephine, who in September, 1880, became my wife, and Lewis, almost from early childhood, and Mrs. Baker was naturally interested in my career.

After the first night of *Kit*, Chanfrau returned to her house, where he was stopping, and Mrs. Baker asked him how I was.

JOSEPHINE BAKER (MRS. JOHN DREW)

"Oh, very bad," he answered.

Each night thereafter she would ask him and he would say: "Worse."

Finally, one night without being questioned, he exploded: "Oh, worse than ever. There is a red-headed girl that he is making love to so much of the time that he cannot remember his cues."

The red-headed girl was Ada Rehan's sister and, while talking to her in the wings, I had missed a very important cue. My part in *The Arkansas Traveler* was that of *Lord Fitzfoley*, one of those preposterous imitations of a traveling Englishman with an equally preposterous valet.

Chanfrau, as *Kit*, was in a violent bowie-knife fight with *Manuel Bond*, the bad man of the piece. I was to fire the shot from off stage which kills the bad man. There was no shot, and he was forced to die without it.

To record that Chanfrau was annoyed is to put the matter mildly.

The next season Ada Rehan went to Albany to play, and I to New York. Charles Morton, the stage manager of the Arch Street Theatre, had written a play, called *Women of the Day*. In this I had a very fine, light comedy rôle, and Daly seems to have been im-

CHAPTER FIVE

WHEN I joined the company at the Fifth Avenue Theatre, Augustin Daly was in the late thirties. He had been in theatrical management about thirteen years and had already had a varied, if not always successful, career. With his own play, *Under the Gaslight*—the first play in which a person is tied to the railroad tracks only to be released just as the locomotive appears on the stage—he had made considerable money at the Old New York Theatre. In 1875 he was confirmed in his ideas, and he possessed the courage of his convictions to an extraordinary degree. He was always willing to fight for the things he wanted, and he had a determination that seemed at variance with his slight build.

Even at this time Daly had adopted the famous black hat which he wore upon all occasions. The somewhat conical shape of the crown accentuated his slimness. These hats seem to have been standardized, and one followed another without noticeable change. Richard, Daly's faithful black servant, who had

JAMES LEWIS AND JOHN DREW IN AUGUSTIN DALY'S PLAY, "PIQUE"

nothing special to do in the theatre and was seldom out of it, received the discarded hats. Years after Daly was dead I noticed one of these on a figure ahead of me in Sixth Avenue. It was Richard, and he still held his head very proudly.

During the early rehearsals of *The Big Bonanza*, Daly was often impatient with the actors. He was tireless in the theatre and seldom went elsewhere. He was an excellent producer of plays, and he knew how to manage his stage. I think that his countless rehearsals had much to do with the smoothness of the plays, for by the time a play reached production, it was cut and dried and there was no need for a tryout at Atlantic City or some other place near New York to find out what the play was like.

Jim Lewis used to refer often to a conversation that he said he had with Daly.

"And where would you be if you weren't in the theatre rehearsing?" the manager was supposed to have asked.

"Oh, out somewhere enjoying ourselves," was Lewis' reply in the conversation that he had invented.

As a matter of fact, we were all young and there was no reason whatever why we should not have rehearsed at ten o'clock every day. But if in dealing with us he was not always patient, Daly did have the

agreeable freedom from affectation and a frank and welcome heartiness of style were perceptible in his effort here and augured well for his future." *The Evening Mail's* comment was: "He acts with intelligence and energy and although by no means a paragon gives promise of marked excellence."

Daly had adapted *The Big Bonanza* from the German play *Ultimo*, by Von Mosher. He had made many adaptations from the German, and it was from this source that he got some of his biggest successes in later years, *Nancy and Company*, *A Night Off*, and *The Railroad of Love*. This play brought together three of the performers who were later to be associated in so many plays, Mrs. Gilbert, James Lewis and myself. With the addition of Ada Rehan we later became what was jestingly known as "The Big Four"—named from the railroad. The program of the Fifth Avenue Theatre contained this announcement:

The Big Bonanza is the second of the series of contemporaneous comedies with which Mr. Daly follows his season of old comedy revivals. The comedy is placed upon the stage under Mr. Daly's personal superintendence, with new scenery, new toilettes, new furniture, and appointments. The cast embraces the favorite artists of the company, and introduces to the New York public Mr. John Drew, who, aside from his own merits, ought to be welcome on account of the fame of his mother, the celebrated Philadelphia actress and manageress, and the memory of his father, who was one of the Irish comedians of the day.

During the run of *The Big Bonanza* the Daly Company played a special holiday matinee in Philadelphia and returned to play the night performance as usual. According to *The Philadelphia Age* the trip was made "without accident of any sort."

In June, Daly decided, having made a pronounced success with *The Big Bonanza*, to make a trip across the continent. Chicago was our first stop. We took with us, not only our New York success, but a number of other plays. There was Boucicault's *London Assurance;* Byron's *Weak Women*, which had been done by the company before I joined; a popular farce, *The Rough Diamond;* Gilbert's *Charity*, and a version of *Oliver Twist*. Fanny Davenport was very fond of the last two, as they gave her character rôles which were a contrast to the well-dressed, light-comedy characters that made up most of the Daly repertoire. On this tour we also played Bronson Howard's famous play, *Saratoga*, with which, under the title of *Brighton*, Charles Wyndham made so great a hit in England.

San Francisco in 1875 was a live town. We stayed

at the Occidental, and on July twelfth we opened with *London Assurance* in Platt's Hall. According to the playbill of that night, this play was to be "As represented at the Fifth Avenue Theatre to crowded and laughter-convulsed audiences." Also from the playbill: "The new scenery to be unfolded this evening will be found in Act 2—The park, and in Act 3—Oak Hall, Gloucestershire." It turned out that there was little room for all this scenery and after two nights we moved to Emerson's Minstrel Hall.

The Big Bonanza was not a success here, for Crane and James O'Neill had already played another version of the same play. We visited Chinatown and saw some of the interminable plays in the Chinese Theatre, at least we were told that one of the plays that we saw had still some days to go. Outwardly Chinatown was a very different place from the place that I saw on numerous later trips.

In San Francisco I met John McCullough, who was running the California Theatre on regular stock lines, playing the usual plays that were popular at the time. On this first trip I met John Mackay, the father of Clarence Mackay, and James Fair, of the celebrated mining outfit, Mackay, Fair, Flood and O'Brien. They owned the Consolidated Virginia Mine in Virginia City, Nevada.

IN THIS GROUP ARE MRS. GILBERT, MISS DAVENPORT, MISS JEFFRYS LEWIS, JAMES LEWIS, AUGUSTIN DALY, AND JOHN DREW, MADE UP IN WORKING CLOTHES, AT THE ENTRANCE TO THE CONSOLIDATED VIRGINIA MINE

From Theatre Collection, Harvard University.

FANNY DAVENPORT

We visited the mine, and there is a picture of Mrs. Gilbert, Miss Davenport, Miss Jeffrys Lewis, James Lewis, Augustin Daly and myself at the entrance to the mine, all made-up in workingmen's clothes. We went down to the depth of some two thousand feet, and then to some lower level on a very small lift. It was very warm in this big silver mine, and Mr. Fair had a man following us with iced champagne and we stopped to partake now and then.

Virginia City was really impressive to us in those days. It was crude and new, and the streets were crowded with men; but they were most deferential and respectful to the women of our company. There was an Indian reservation near there, and we saw a fight between a white man and an Indian. Neither had any idea of science, but the crowd did not seem to mind, and the combatants dealt each other horrible blows. The white man finally overcame the Indian who, we were assured, was in no way hostile, and the fight was purely a personal affair.

On our way back East we played in Salt Lake City. The theatre, which had been built in the late fifties or early sixties, was a very fine one. I have played in the same house many times since, and it has always been, as then, well run and well cared for; but in those days it had a big, fine green room, which was later changed into a dressing room. In this theatre, when it was the home of a stock company, Maude Adams' mother, whose real name was Kiskadden, played leading women for many years.

Curiously enough, the play selected for our opening bill in Salt Lake City was Bronson Howard's *Saratoga*. Elsewhere the complications resulting from the pursuit of the hero, *Bob Sackett*, by three infatuated women had been considered excruciatingly funny, but the Mormons, as Brigham Young himself pointed out to us, would have solved a problem like *Sackett's* so easily that there would have been no play.

The day after we opened, Miss Davenport, Mrs. Gilbert, Jim Lewis and Mrs. Lewis, Daly and I went to call upon Brigham Young, who gave us a sort of audience at his official residence. He seemed a familiar figure and looked very much like his pictures, except that he was older and somewhat feeble, and he had a growth or goiter that was said to have been caused by drinking snow water from the mountains. Of course this must have been false, for the water was perfectly pellucid.

He expressed a great deal of interest in our work and particularly in the play, *Saratoga*. "But why," he asked, turning to Lewis, who played the part of

Bob Sackett, the pursued hero, "should the author have made such a complication out of the efforts of your character to get away from the three women who are in love with him?"

Jim Lewis was somewhat puzzled by the question. "What else," he asked, "could *Sackett* do but try to escape?"

"Marry them all," was Brigham Young's answer.

He said this so seriously that none of us knew whether he meant his solution as a wheeze or not, and we talked of other things.

He told us that when he was a young man he could speak with such distinctness and with so much volume that he could be heard for great distances. I hesitate to guess now what these figures were, but they were very impressive, even taking into consideration the rarified atmosphere. Our visit to Brigham Young was not so profitable in experience, nor did it yield so much material as Artemus Ward got out of his visit to the Mormons.

The manager of the hotel in Salt Lake City provided us with excellent horses, and we rode round on these to see the surrounding country. We visited Camp Douglas, which had been established as an army post when the Mormons proved rebellious. It was here that I first met General Sheridan, who was then on a tour of inspection.

Before we left we played *The Rough Diamond*, and the Salt Lake City papers made much of a line that Lewis interpolated. As I looked young for the character I was to play, I made up with a very elaborate beard.

As I came on the stage Lewis who had a way of interpolating lines naturally and still letting the audience in on the joke, said: "Here comes the Prince of Wales." He who was later Edward the Seventh had made the wearing of a beard the fashion in the early seventies and the jest, though feeble, went well in Salt Lake City.

I remember another occasion, some years afterward, when Lewis, annoyed at having to play on Sunday in Chicago, took a great many liberties with the text of his part. The seats down front were all occupied by circus people, who did not have to work on Sunday. They had come to see a former colleague, Miss Rose Stokes, who appeared in one scene where there was a Maypole dance. She had been a rider, but after an accident had given up the tanbark ring for the stage.

Charles Fisher played an old man and wore white, muttonchop sidewhiskers. He was just about to make a dignified entrance when Lewis who was on the stage called to him, "Walk right in, Mr. Forepaugh."

The circus people were delighted and stopped the play for some minutes. In truth, Fisher looked not unlike the dignified kindly old gentleman whose pictures adorned circus bills for many years.

CHAPTER SIX

IN October of that year we—that is, the Daly Company—appeared with Edwin Booth. The season had been postponed, as Booth had been thrown from a carriage, and when he first appeared at rehearsals his arm was in a sling. In *Hamlet*, Charles Fisher was *Polonius*; William Davidge, the *Grave Digger*; Harkins, the *Ghost*; Hardenberg, the *King*; Maurice Barrymore, who was soon after to be my brother-in-law, *Laertes*; Jeffrys Lewis, *Ophelia*; and Alice Grey, the *Queen*. I played *Rosencrantz*.

Of my performance the only criticism I can remember is that of William Winter, who wrote: "The gentleman who played *Rosencrantz* evidently had an engagement with a friend after the performance, so hurried was his speech and so evident his desire to get through with his part." In those days I was very much inclined to speak too rapidly.

Of that long cast only Jeffrys Lewis and I are alive today. A few years ago, when *The Scrap of Paper* was staged at the Empire Theatre, Miss Lewis played

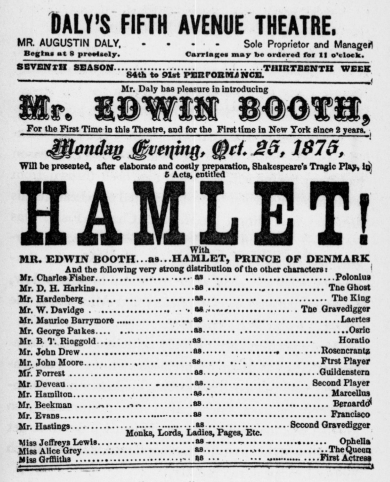

DALY'S FIFTH AVENUE THEATRE,

MR. AUGUSTIN DALY, - - - - Sole Proprietor and Manager

Begins at 8 precisely. **Carriages may be ordered for 11 o'clock.**

SEVENTH SEASON..............................THIRTEENTH WEEK
84th to 91st PERFORMANCE.

Mr. Daly has pleasure in introducing

Mr. EDWIN BOOTH,

For the First Time in this Theatre, and for the First time in New York since 2 years.

Monday Evening, Oct. 25, 1875,

Will be presented, after elaborate and costly preparation, Shakespeare's Tragic Play, in
5 Acts, entitled

HAMLET!

With
MR. EDWIN BOOTH...as...HAMLET, PRINCE OF DENMARK
And the following very strong distribution of the other characters:

Mr. Charles Fisher	as	Polonius
Mr. D. H. Harkins	as	The Ghost
Mr. Hardenberg	as	The King
Mr. W. Davidge	as	The Gravedigger
Mr. Maurice Barrymore	as	Laertes
Mr. George Parkes	as	Osric
Mr. B. T. Ringgold	as	Horatio
Mr. John Drew	as	Rosencrantz
Mr. John Moore	as	First Player
Mr. Forrest	as	Guildenstern
Mr. Deveau	as	Second Player
Mr. Hamilton	as	Marcellus
Mr. Beekman	as	Bernardo
Mr. Evans	as	Francisco
Mr. Hastings	as	Second Gravedigger

Monks, Lords, Ladies, Pages, Etc.

Miss Jeffreys Lewis	as	Ophelia
Miss Alice Grey	as	The Queen
Miss Grffiiths	as	First Actress

IN "HAMLET" WITH BOOTH

55

During rehearsals I made the same mistake several times. Edwin Booth was, as always, gentle and kind, and fortunately when the actual performance came I spoke the line correctly.

I played *Francis*, in *The Stranger*, with Booth. *Francis* is what is known in the business as a "liny" part. By that we mean that the speeches are very short, broken lines. They have no semblance of continuity and are constantly interrupted by the other characters. Almost every actor, particularly the young actor, has had difficulties with a part of the sort. When I played *Francis* with Booth I had a good memory, and I thought that I had mastered the broken speeches. During the performance I tripped a number of times, and when I apologized to Booth afterwards he was very gentle, very nice. He patted me on the shoulder. Evidently he had been through it himself, or perhaps he had seen many others go wrong in this thankless rôle.

I thought that I had done with *The Stranger* forever, but some years after, in London, Maurice Barrymore and I went to Kings Cross Station to take a train for the country. We were ahead of time and near the station was a small theatre with alluring bills. We decided to kill half an hour with *Walberg, the Avenger*. The play was on when we entered, and it seemed strangely familiar. It turned out to be the old fashioned play, *The Stranger*. Barrymore remembered that in this piece one of the characters refers to *The Stranger* by his right name which was *Walberg*. The actor playing this character was unusually bad and suggested the actor in W. S. Gilbert's ballad "who mouthed and mugged in simulated rage."

After the engagement with Booth I played with Adelaide Neilson in *Twelfth Night* and *Cymbeline*. In the latter play I was *Cloten*, which is supposed to be the comedy part: it wasn't—as I played it. After my head is supposed to be cut off *Imogen* discovers my body and thinking that it is her husband, *Posthumous*, throws herself upon me. It was rather uncomfortable, as my head was covered with some dusty grass mats. My discomfiture was added to on the first night by the fact that I could tell that Miss Neilson was laughing.

"What was the matter?" I asked her immediately afterwards.

She merely continued to laugh.

"Did my head show, or was something wrong with my costume?"

"Oh, no, everything was all right," she told me; "but I once played that scene with a very portly *Cloten*, and when I threw myself upon him I rebounded and bounced. I have never been able to play that scene, serious though it is, without laughing under my breath."

Things had been going very badly with Daly for some time, and he lost the Fifth Avenue Theatre. I played with my mother's old friend, Joseph Jefferson, in *Rip Van Winkle* for a while at Booth's Theatre, which was at Sixth Avenue and Twenty-third Street. At first I was the innkeeper, *Seth*, who chalks up drinks for *Rip* at the beginning of the play and later I was *Henrick Vedder*, the sailor, who comes in on the fourth act, when *Rip* has reappeared after his sleep. This part is played by a child in the first act.

The next summer, with my old friend of Philadelphia days, Lewis Baker, I went abroad. That was the year of the exposition at Paris, and all the boats were crowded. We were very much on the cheap and sailed on an inferior boat of a Scotch line.

In London we saw Herman Vezin play a dramatization of "The Vicar of Wakefield" called *Olivia*. Vezin was an American, born in Philadelphia, but he was always identified with the English stage and never played here. This same play, *Olivia*, by W. G. Wills, was later played by Henry Irving, who was then playing his wonderful melodramatic success, *The Bells*.

In Paris we saw Sarah Bernhardt play *L'Etrangère*, at the Comédie Française with Coquelin, Mounet-Sully and the other fine actors of that great theatre. This play was later done in New York by Daly under the title of *The American*.

On our return to England we saw the Columbia four-oar crew win the Stewards' Cup at Henley. The only friend we met on this trip was J. S. Clarke, who then had the lease of the Haymarket Theatre. He had been associated with my father in Philadelphia. He made quite a success as a comedian in London, but he was not acting when Baker and I met him.

When we got home I went directly to Philadelphia, where I played *Charles Surface* for the first time, in the screen scene in *The School for Scandal*, at the Arch Street Theatre. The occasion was a benefit for a local charity. In order to play *Charles*, I shaved off my mustache, and this has been considered on the part of some actors a great sacrifice. It was especially so regarded in the seventies. Edwin Forrest, as his pictures will show, never would remove his side whiskers no matter what the period or the character.

CHAPTER SEVEN

I NEXT went on tour with my brother-in-law, Maurice Barrymore. He and Frederick Warde had purchased the road rights to the great Wallack's Theatre success, *Diplomacy*. I was engaged to play the juvenile part, *Algie Fairfax*. As the venture was not proving profitable, Warde and Barrymore, a short time after we had gone on tour, decided to split. Warde was to take part of the company and go West. Barrymore was to keep some of the actors, engage a few additional ones, and play the Southern territory.

I stayed with Barrymore and from then on played the part of *Henry Beauclerc*, which had, up to this time, been played by Warde. Maurice Barrymore played *Julian Beauclerc*, the younger brother. H. Rees Davies, an actor of considerable experience, was *Baron Stein* and Ben Porter played *Count Orloff*. Porter was a good-looking man in the early forties, who had played in the Furbish Company which did for a time the old Daly play, *Divorce*. *Countess Zicka* was played by Ellen Cummings, an attractive young

AN EARLY PICTURE OF MAURICE BARRYMORE

woman who had been in the Louisville Stock Company. In this same company Ada Rehan had played for a time after the days at the Arch Street Theatre and before her engagement by Augustin Daly.

It was on this tour—at Marshall, Texas—that Ben Porter was killed and Barrymore severely wounded. We had played at the Opera House that night in March, the sixth anniversary of my appearance on the stage, and were waiting for a train to take us to Texarkana.

We were stopping at the Station Hotel, and most of us went directly there after the play; but Barrymore, Porter and Miss Cummings decided to have something to eat, and they went to the only lunch room that was open, the one at the station.

This lunch room was a sort of bar as well. One man was waiting on both parts of the room. A man named Jim Curry, an employee of the railroad and a deputy sheriff, began using offensive language and affronted Miss Cummings.

Barrymore demanded that he stop.

"I can do any of you up," said Curry.

"I suppose you could," answered Barrymore, "with your pistol or knife."

"I haven't got any pistol or knife. I'll do it with

my bunch of fives," said Curry, as he proudly displayed a fist like a sledge hammer.

"Then," said Barrymore, throwing off his coat, "I'll have a go at you."

But Curry did have a gun and he shot Barrymore, wounding him in the shoulder. When Porter rushed to Barrymore's aid, Curry shot him. Porter died almost immediately, on the station platform.

I heard the shooting at the hotel, and I ran along the station platform and entered the only place that was lighted, the lunch room. As I entered, the man with the gun grabbed me. Why he did not shoot I do not know. In another minute or two the sheriff of Marshall arrived, took the gun away from his deputy and locked him up.

We stayed on in Marshall for some days, till Barrymore was out of danger. When the physician showed him the ball that had been cut out of the muscle of his back, Barrymore said: "I'll give it to my son Lionel to cut his teeth on."

Our hotel at the station was some distance from the town itself, and the next night when I was going to the druggist's to get a prescription filled for Barrymore, the train dispatcher called me aside and said: "You'd better take my pistol."

I did so and walked along the dark road to the town with some little apprehension. The shooting at the lunch room had made us rather conspicuous in Marshall.

There was only one house lighted along the road and when I was just opposite that a woman called to me: "Where are you going?"

I told her: "To the druggist's, and then back to the hotel."

She said: "When you go back to the station will you tell my husband, he's train dispatcher"—the very man who had given me the gun—"that there are some tramps hanging around here. They've been in here to demand food."

I went on to the druggist's, obtained the medicine and started back on the long, dark road, now without a single light. The pistol gave me confidence of a sort, but of course I didn't want to use it; I never had used one.

With my hand on the gun, which was in my side pocket, I looked anxiously at the one or two persons I met on the way. When I returned the pistol to its owner I told him of his wife's fears, and he and another man went up to his house and apprehended two men who were put in jail. And though I had been anxious along the road, happily there were no other casualties during our visit to Marshall.

The people of Texas, to show their detestation of the whole affair and their sympathy with the company, offered us the hospitality of a number of towns that no touring company would have thought of visiting. I do not suppose these towns would have been especially attractive or profitable for a "one-man show" at that time. Mesquite was one of these, and Eagle Ford another. We were promised good houses; but of course we could not play *Diplomacy* with two of our leading characters missing.

We played two or three farces, which we studied for the occasion. One of these was an old piece called *The Little Treasure.* In this the property man played a young English fop. He wore clothes of Barrymore's that didn't fit him, and a light-yellow wig that slipped badly and either showed his dark hair at the temple or at the neck in back. This was a sort of "town hall tonight" tour. When there was no theatre, we played in a hall and once in the dining room of a hotel.

Curry was twice brought to trial, but acquitted. There were witnesses in court to testify that Curry had shot Porter and Barrymore in self-defense. As a matter of fact, at the time of the shooting there was no one in the lunch room except the participants and the man who was waiting upon them. He was spirited away and never appeared in court.

The night of the second acquittal Barrymore, who had twice gone to Texas at great expense and inconvenience, was sitting in front of the hotel—this time the hotel in town—airing his views upon Texas justice. In no mincing words he was telling a citizen of the place what he thought.

Just then a man walked past them into the hotel.

"Do you know who that was?" asked Barrymore's companion.

"No."

"That was the lawyer who defended Curry."

Barrymore leaned back and heard the lawyer ask the hotel clerk in a voice that sounded truculent to him: "Is Mr. Maurice Barrymore here?"

"He's right outside," said the clerk.

The lawyer came out and stood in the light from the door and asked: "Is Maurice Barrymore here?"

Barrymore who noticed that the lawyer had his hand on his hip pocket declared himself present a little reluctantly. He thought that there might be another shooting imminent.

"Here," said the lawyer, taking his gun from his pocket and holding the butt out to Barrymore, "is the pistol that killed Porter and wounded you."

CHAPTER EIGHT

WHILE I was in Texas, Daly had been abroad, where he bought the rights to the play made from Zola's famous book, "L'Assommoir." Under the title of *Drink*, in a version written by Charles Reade, this play was done by Charles Warner for five thousand nights in England. In New York, when produced by Daly at the Olympic Theatre, it was a complete failure and ran only a short time. In the cast were Maude Granger, Emily Rigl, B. T. Ringold, Frank Sanger; my uncle, Frank Drew; and Ada Rehan. Gardner, the manager of the Arch Street Theatre, had recommended Ada Rehan to Daly, and in this play she played for the first time under his management. Olive Logan, who wrote the play *Surf*, which had a record run at the Arch Street Theatre and had also been produced by Daly, made the version American in all respects, but not sufficiently different to account for the failure here and the great success when played by Warner.

This failure did not discourage Daly or his chief backer, John Duff, his father-in-law, and they set out

ADA REHAN AND JOHN DREW IN "DOLLARS AND SENSE"

to find a new theatre early in 1879. On the West side of Broadway between Twenty-ninth and Thirtieth streets was an old building which had been Banvard's and later Wood's Museum. Downstairs was an exhibition hall which was chiefly famous as the place where the Cardiff giant was displayed.

The auditorium was up a flight of steps and very small. Daly's architect contrived by a series of steps some feet apart to give the impression when the place was made over that the theatre was on the ground floor. As a matter of fact, the stage had been lowered somewhat and a new proscenium arch made. Because the building was old and so far out of the theatrical district the rental was low. There was great pessimism over the location of the theatre, so far uptown.

When he had finished the physical changes in the theatre and had redecorated the whole, Daly gathered together a company. As in the opening of the Fifth Avenue Theatre, he selected mostly young players. After some correspondence and a visit or two I was engaged. I asked for forty dollars a week, but Daly would only give me thirty-five.

In a letter I had written him I mentioned that since the Fifth Avenue Theatre days I had had quite a little experience and had improved in my enunciation. He wrote me that he was glad to hear that I had improved

though at night it is light enough. A door opens
into one end of the property-room—a place where
all sorts of things are kept that are used on the
stage—and through that we pass out to the stage.

At the time of the opening Daly's theatre was, of
course, lighted by gas. The flames were protected by
wire netting and the jets were lighted by spark. Later,
when electric lighting was first installed, there was no
plant in the theatre, the supply coming from the city
power house.

Often the lights would go out, and the explanation
was always that they were changing a belt.

It was not very reassuring for the audiences to sit in
darkness; nor was it comfortable for the players, who
had come to a complete standstill on the stage and
were waiting for the lights to come on.

From the beginning Daly was insistent that no one
should be allowed back stage on first nights. As a matter of fact, it was impossible to get to the stage or
dressing rooms at any time, so zealously was the door
to the stage guarded by a large, unlettered, rough, but
kindly Hibernian, named Owen Gormley.

He seemed very surly; but of course he was only
doing what Daly wanted him to do, and he did keep
people out of the theatre. Owen could not read, and
he regarded everyone who presented a letter or card

JOHN DREW AND WILLIAM GILBERT IN "RED LETTER NIGHTS"

with a good deal of suspicion. It was hopeless to try to get mail from him.

Owen had the distinction of having kept Mark Twain out of the theatre when he came by special appointment to see Daly. After the one-hundredth performance of *The Taming of the Shrew*, Daly gave a supper at a large round table on the stage of the theatre. Twain was introduced by General Sherman, and we then heard, for the first time, how Owen had kept him from his appointment.

Twain began by saying: "This is the hardest theatre in New York to get into, even at the front door." He then went on and described in an excruciatingly funny way his encounter with Owen after he had found his way through the long hallway into the backyard which led to the stage.

The first night of Daly's theatre was really not an auspicious occasion. Daly had failed so completely with the Fifth Avenue Theatre, and his attempt to come back with *L'Assommoir* had been so unfortunate that perhaps at no time in his career of management did his name mean so little to the public as when he opened his own theatre on September 18, 1879.

Nor was the opening bill a success. There was a one-act play called *Love's Young Dream*, in which Ada Rehan, May Fielding, Charles Fisher and George

Parkes appeared. This was followed by *Newport*, subtitled *The Swimmer, The Singer and The Cipher*. According to the program I was *Tom Sanderson*, a master bather with an overmastering secret. The cast was:

HON. PETER PORTER	Charles Leclercq
HON. U. B. BLODE	William Davidge
BEN BOULGATE	Hart Conway
CAPT. CHICKERING	George Parkes
TOM SANDERSON	John Drew
CAPTAIN BLACKWELL	Frank Iredale
CRUTCH REYNOLDS	Walter Edmunds
UNDO	Frank V. Bennett
TOGGS	Maggie Barnes
MIDGET	Laura Thorpe
THOMPSON	Earle Stirling
GINGER	E. Wilkes
OFFICER	P. Hunting
HON. MRS. PETER PORTER	Catherine Lewis
THE WIDOW WARBOYS	Mrs. Charles Poole
MISS BELLE BLODE	Georgine Flagg
COSETTE	Annie Wakeman

In this comedy with songs Olive Logan had attempted to repeat the success which she had attained with her earlier play about a fashionable summer resort, *Surf*. She failed to get from *Newport* what she had found in the background of Cape May and the public stayed away from the new theatre.

Divorce, a success of a few years before, was revived

as soon as possible and rehearsals begun on a new
play by Bronson.Howard called *Wives*. This was an
adaptation from Molière's two plays, *L'Ecole des
Femmes* and *L'Ecole des Maris* and so far as I can
ascertain this is the first time that Molière, so often
adapted and borrowed from, was given credit on an
American playbill.

The cast for this five-act comedy produced October
18, 1879, was:

ARNOLPHE, Marquis of Fontenoy	Charles Fisher
SCANARELLE LAMARRE	William Davidge
VICOMTE ARISTE	George Morton
CHRISALDE	John Drew
HORACE DE CHATEAUROUX	Harry Lacy
CAPTAIN FIEREMONTE	George Parkes
DORIVAL	Hart Conway
ALAIN	Charles Leclercq
JEAN JACQUES	F. Bennett
CAPTAIN BALLANDER	W. Edmunds
THE COMMISSARY	Mr. Hunting
THE NOTARY	Mr. Sterling
AGNES	Catherine Lewis
ISABELLE DE NESLE	Ada Rehan
LENORA DE NESLE	Margaret Lanner
LISETTE	Maggie Harold
GEORGETTE	Sydney Nelson

During this first season neither James Lewis nor
Mrs. Gilbert was in the company, and it was not till

the following September that we were all cast together in a play called *Our First Families*, by Edgar Fawcett.

The playbills at Daly's theatre always had a synopsis with the character. Thus, in *An Arabian Night*, I was *Mr. Alexander Spinkle*, "a retired broker and ex-Caliph; a devoted young husband with a fatal passion for the Arabian Nights." And Ada Rehan was *Miss Kate Spinkle*, "an American girl brought up abroad, and astonished at the ways at home." In *The Way We Live* I was *Clyde Monograme* "who lives the best way he can since his wife lives for everybody else." And Ada Rehan was *Cherry Monograme*, "who lives in her carriage and makes short calls at home."

Both of these were plays which Daly had adapted from the German. In the first I had the sort of light comedy part that I played so often in the Daly Theatre and in the second Ada Rehan and I played opposite each other as we were to do for so many years afterward.

At the end of the season we opened a spring tour in Boston with *An Arabian Night*. This rather light comedy did not fill the vast spaces of the Boston Theatre. On the first night a pony that was brought on in one of the scenes stepped on my foot and cracked my patent-leather shoe. Otherwise this visit to Boston was quite uneventful, except that it gave me an opportunity to call upon that fine actor, William Warren. He was an old friend of my mother's and had been associated at one time or another with other members of the family.

I never had the good fortune to act with him. At the time I visited him he was the idol of the Boston Museum, where he played for many years.

I called upon him at Miss Amelia Fisher's boarding house in Bullfinch Place, where he was a perpetual guest and liked by everyone. To call Miss Fisher's house a theatrical boarding house is not a fair description, for it was really a delightful place and nothing at all like the boarding house which Helen Green has celebrated under the name of "Maison de Shine."

I talked to William Warren of our play. He sympathized with our company for having to play so frothy a piece in so huge a theatre. "It is like," he said, "trying to tell a funny story across the Common."

A great many members of the profession did not care to stay at Miss Fisher's because she never gave her guests a latch key, but would sit up and wait for them to come home. She always let her guests in herself. I can remember when Charlie Stevenson went to Boston. He thought that it would be fine to stay there where so many of the profession had been. It had always seemed so pleasant when he had visited friends who were living in Miss Fisher's house. But he felt the restraint when he lived there himself. He did not want to keep the old lady sitting up for him after the theatre, and he did not want to come home on cue.

CHAPTER NINE

THE second season of Daly's opened with *Tiote*, a romantic melodrama with the scene laid in Wales. It was a prompt failure. Then came *Our First Families*, which brought together the four players who were to be associated through the eighties and early nineties.

Mrs. Gilbert was an old dear. Even in the days of the Fifth Avenue Company we called her "Grandma." Ada Rehan was handsome and attractive. She was big, whole-hearted, good-natured and one of the most lovable of women. She had fine, expressive eyes, which counted much in the theatre.

Jim Lewis was the most companionable of men, and I never had a better friend. There is no use discussing his great talent and his great ability. That does not mean much now, but there is a story concerning him which means much to me. The summer before I played *Rosemary* we were all living together at West Hampton, Long Island—the Lewises, Henry Miller and his family, my mother, the Barrymore children and my wife, daughter and myself. Lewis saw a Sunday

From Theatre Collection, Harvard University.

A TYPICAL DALY COMEDY FROM THE GERMAN WITH "THE BIG FOUR" IN THE CAST

paper in which a certain writer of theatrical affairs drew a rather personal comparison between my acting and that of Charles Wyndham, who had played *Rosemary* in London. It was the conviction of the writer of this article that the part of *Sir Jasper* was too serious for me and somewhat beyond my depth; in fact, that I should fail in *Rosemary*. Lewis took the trouble to cut this out of all the copies of the paper in the house so that I would not see the disparaging remarks while I was studying the part I was to play the last of August at the Empire Theatre, and so that my family would not see them. It was most thoughtful and so characteristic of Lewis! As a matter of fact, *Rosemary* was a big success.

The second season at Daly's had not started out too bravely, but when *Needles and Pins* was produced the success of this theatre, so far above the theatrical district, seemed to be assured. *Needles and Pins* was an adaptation of Rosen's *Starke Mitteln*. It had a run of a hundred nights. Miss Rehan and I played opposite each other. She was a young girl in her 'teens, and I a young lawyer captivated by her youthful charm. Mrs. Gilbert played one of those elderly spinsters trying to grow young, and James Lewis was an elderly bachelor in love with her.

From this second season of the new Daly's Ada Rehan was an assured success. E. A. Dithmar at a somewhat later date wrote: "Miss Ada Rehan has no lack of appreciation and she is growing in her art. Her record belongs to the future; but it has been interesting and profitable to watch her artistic work from the days of *Needles and Pins*, in which Miss Rehan as a kittenish girl acted as a mediator in the mature romance of a bald and bashful bachelor and a gushing yet timid spinster, portrayed by Mr. Lewis and Mrs. Gilbert."

The plot of *Needles and Pins* was complicated and sentimental, and it was not a play that could live any number of years in any theatre, but the comedy scenes were genuine good fun. I suppose that its most conspicuous merit was that it was unlike anything to be seen elsewhere in New York at that time. It belonged to the group of plays that Daly adapted from the German. Some were better than others, but the standard did not change much. They were always very pleasing, light and clean.

The company and the performances were beginning to attract attention and it was somewhere around this time that Mark Twain and other people prominent in literature and art began to come to the theatre. I remember that Mark Twain told me in those early

From Theatre Collection, Harvard University.

OTIS SKINNER, ADA REHAN, JAMES LEWIS, MRS. G. H. GILBERT, AND JOHN DREW, IN "THE RAILROAD OF LOVE," ONE OF DALY'S MANY COMEDIES FROM THE GERMAN

days that he had thought of writing a play for the Daly Company. It was a grand, brilliant and original idea. At least so he thought when he began to work upon it. The play was a dream play, and in the end it all came out right and the disasters that happened in the play were mere distortions of the imagination. Before submitting the play to Daly he thought that he would take it to some friend who knew something about dramatic construction; so he submitted the manuscript to Sinclair McKelway of the *Brooklyn Eagle*.

All this Twain told me with that characteristic drawl which, had anyone perfected and imitated it on the stage, would have been labeled at once as downright impossible.

When Twain got his play back from his friend there was no comment, just a list of the hundreds of different plays from 400 B. C. to the time he was writing which had had this same original idea of violent happenings that turn out to be merely dreams.

With *Needles and Pins*, then, we had settled down to the success and prosperity which lasted all through the eighties. It was less than eight years before that Ada Rehan and I had played together for the first time on the stage of the Arch Street Theatre. With all the praise and attention that were showered upon her Ada

Rehan's point of view never changed. She was always the same unaffected, natural person of the early days.

I felt that I had made quite an impression, and I am afraid that I conveyed this idea to Joseph Jefferson in a talk that I had with him. He was an old friend of my mother's and I think that he, with the best of good nature, took upon himself the task of correcting any false idea I might have about my position in the theatre.

To point a moral and to convince me that, however big I might think myself, there was certain to be some one a little bigger, he told me that when he had made his great success with *Rip Van Winkle*—the play that was to immortalize him and that he was to do everywhere for years to come—he thought himself fairly important and that everyone knew of his success. At the very least he felt that he had put Washington Irving on the map with this Boucicault version of *Rip*.

One night, after the theatre, as he was going to his room in the Fifth Avenue Hotel, a stockily built man with a grizzly beard got into the elevator.

"Are you playing in town now, Mr. Jefferson?" he asked.

Jefferson, as he replied in the affirmative, rather pitied the man for his ignorance and his total lack of understanding of what was going on in the world.

What a simpleton he must be who did not know that
Rip was having a record run!

When this man reached his floor and got out Jefferson asked the elevator boy: "Who was that?"

"Why," said the boy, in his turn pitying Jefferson
for his ignorance, "that's General Grant!"

man's rôle, but there was precedent for Daly's putting Mrs. Gilbert into the part, as a Mrs. LeBrun had played *Curtis* when Clara Morris played *Katherine* and Louis James *Petruchio* at the Academy of Music some years before. In the whole line of light comedies Mrs. Gilbert and Lewis had played opposite each other, and *Curtis* enabled her to play a low-comedy scene with *Grumio*, which was played by Lewis on this occasion.

At the end of the performance Horace Howard Furness, being already on the stage, was the first to reach us. He congratulated Ada Rehan, the *Katherine*, and me, the *Petruchio*. I do not see how he could have heard any of the play even from his vantage point in the first entrance, for he was so deaf that it was necessary to shout into his ear trumpet.

Katherine was that night, and always remained, the greatest part in Ada Rehan's long list of performances. *Petruchio* was to me the most grateful rôle that I have played. It has everything that the player of high comedy can desire: telling speeches and effective situations; in fact, everything that makes for and makes up a great part. Since *Petruchio* is a great Shakespearian character, it may be imagined how gratifying it was to be told by everyone whose opinion and judgment I

ADA REHAN AS KATHERINE

regarded that I had come out of the effort successfully.

The Taming of the Shrew was really a novelty in 1887. A short version of the play known as *Katherine and Petruchio* had been played by a number of trage-dians when they wanted a rest. This garbled version, which consisted mainly of the horse-play scenes in which *Petruchio* brandishes his whip and the leg of mutton about the stage, had been played by Edwin Booth. It was this version that Clara Morris and Louis James had played; in fact, for stage use the play had come to be known as *Katherine and Petruchio*. The Daly production went back to the play as written and *The Induction* was restored. Presumably, the characters in *The Induction* were then played for the first time in America.

Christopher Sly, a drunken tinker, is observed by a lord and his servants as they are coming from a hunt. *Sly* has been thrown out of an alehouse. It occurs to the lord to dress this fellow up and when he comes round to serve him with all ceremonies and make him believe that he is a great lord. The real lord has his page, a part very well played by the youthful Willie Collier, dress up as a woman and pretend to be the wife of *Sly*. When everything is ready the real lord, dressed as a servant, comes to him and says:

Jaques, Hobart Bosworth, *Charles*, and I was *Orlando*. This was the first appearance of Henrietta Crosman at Daly's Theatre. I had played in a scene from *As You Like It* once before and that was at a benefit for Fanny Davenport at the Fifth Avenue Theatre. On that occasion I played *Jaques de Bois*, the second son of old *Sir Rowland de Bois*. This is a small part and the character only comes on at the end of the play. In that performance Lawrence Barrett was the *Jaques*. Afterwards he came over and talked to me. I had never met him. He had known my father, and he knew my mother.

The following spring we played *As You Like It* on the lawn of the Farwell estate at Lake Forest, near Chicago. It had been raining for many days and the ground was so damp that it was necessary for the women to wear rubbers. It was of course a daylight performance, and we did not know how to make up; that is, adapt our regular make-up for daylight. We appealed to William Gilbert, who had once been with a circus, but as he had been a clown his ideas of make-up were not very helpful to those of us who were supposed to be living in the Forest of Arden.

George Clarke suggested that we use some stuff called bolarmenia. This is a brownish make-up that is used for Indian characters, and he thought that a little

DA REHAN AS ROSALIND, JOHN DREW AS ORLANDO, IN "AS YOU LIKE IT"

of this on our cheeks would give us the healthy appearance of people who live in the open air. He imparted this information with so much assurance that we thought he must know what he was talking about. I went on with this stuff on my face. My appearance in the mirror was not too reassuring, but I fancied that the distance of the spectators from the stage in this beautiful amphitheatre would take care of things and offset to some degree, at least, the strange-looking image that I saw in my mirror.

In the scene where they try to dissuade *Orlando* from wrestling with the great fellow *Charles*, *Celia* has a speech:

> Young gentleman, your spirits are too bold for your years. You have seen cruel proof of this man's strength; if you saw yourself with your eyes or knew yourself with your judgment, the fear of your adventure would counsel you to a more equal enterprise. We pray you, for your own sake, to embrace your own safety and give over this attempt.

During this speech Ada Rehan looked at me for the first time, and apparently she had never seen anything so funny; and she laughed so much that she was scarcely able to give the speech of *Rosalind*:

> Do, young sir; your reputation shall not therefore be misprised; we will make it our suit to the duke that the wrestling might not go forward.

"You looked like an effeminate Indian," she told me afterwards.

My long-haired wig added to this impression. We found out later that George Clarke had just tried out an experiment on us and that he had not played under similar conditions before.

In the wrestling scene upon this occasion Hobart Bosworth, who was the *Charles*—the giant that *Orlando* throws—did not take the ordinary precautions that we took in this scene upon the stage. He thought that the soft, damp ground would protect him. When he was thrown he landed on the point of his shoulder, and it was so painful that he uttered a ringing oath. Fortunately, the distances were so great that he was heard only by the actors. Altogether our open-air performance was not a happy one.

There was an all-star performance of the same play —*As You Like It*—for some charity given on the property of Agnes Booth at Manchester on the Massachusetts coast one summer. Crane, Robson, Frank Mayo, Rose Coghlan and many other famous people were in the cast. Mayo, who was a great popular favorite, was the *Jaques*. He had some very long waits and as it was a very warm day, he had walked over to the hotel for a cooling glass. In the midst of a conversation with a friend, he was interrupted by a call boy. *Jaques* was wanted. It was his great entrance into the Forest of Arden. It was time for the speech, "The Seven Ages of Man." Thinking to save time, he took a short cut, which led over some fences. As he got near where the stage was he began reciting his speech to give the impression that he really wasn't late but was on the job all the time. This is an old dodge, often resorted to in the theatre, but Mayo had not calculated his distances very closely and when he arrived on the scene, panting and breathless, his speech, "The Seven Ages of Man," was all gone.

Love's Labour's Lost was the last of the Shakespearian revivals that I played in at Daly's. After I had left, Ada Rehan played both *Viola* and *Portia*, but *Katherine* was always her great character.

Love's Labour's Lost had been produced by Daly at The Fifth Avenue Theatre in 1874 and at that time, which must have been one of the first productions of this play in New York, Ada Dyas, Fanny Davenport, Davidge, Harkins, Fisher, Louis James and Hart Conway .appeared.

Though his first production of this little acted play was not a success Daly decided to revive it in March, 1891, with this cast:

THE KING OF NAVARRE	John Drew
LONGAVILLE	Hobart Bosworth
DON ADRIANO DE ARMADO	Sidney Herbert
SIR NATHANIEL	Charles Leclercq
HOLOFERNES	Harry Edwards
THE PRINCESS OF FRANCE	Ada Rehan
JACQUENETTA	Kitty Cheatham
BIRON	Geo. Clarke
BOYET	Charles Wheatleigh
MERCADE	Wilfred Buckland
DULL	William Sampson
COSTARD	James Lewis
ROSALINE	Edith Crane
MARIA	Adelaide Prince
MOTH	Flossie Ethel
KATHERINE	Isabel Irving

Willie Collier, who made his first appearance on the stage in Shakespeare, as the page in *The Induction* of *The Taming of the Shrew*, came into the theatre as a call boy. Even as a boy he had an extraordinary manner of saying perfectly absurd and ridiculous things with the utmost seriousness. Lewis, a comedian himself, took the greatest delight in Collier and encouraged him greatly. Collier was an excellent mimic, and his imitation of Daly was uncanny.

One day Collier was talking to Lewis and myself in a dressing room and imitating Daly. John Moore, the stage manager, was looking for Daly to consult him about something upon which an immediate decision

JOHN DREW AS THE KING OF NAVARRE IN "LOVE'S LABOUR'S LOST"

was required.   He heard Daly talking in our dressing room.   He stood aghast outside the door, for the things that the supposed Daly was saying were unlike anything that Daly could possibly have said.   The matter was urgent, and he had to interrupt.   When he knocked and entered and found that Daly really wasn't there he was so dazed that he left the room without a word.

We never heard further from the incident, but we impressed upon Collier that he must keep his imitations of Daly for our ears alone.   Lewis enjoyed them so much that he was loath to give them up altogether.

We were all very sorry when Willie Collier left the company.   I was especially so, because it broke up our baseball club.   He was a capital pitcher and an extremely good organizer.   We had no catcher and usually recruited someone from the property room of the theatre we were playing to fill that position.   Sometimes a scene shifter received Collier's delivery.   Steve Murphy, who later, as Steve Grattan, played a number of parts at the old Lyceum, was really a good first baseman.   Otis Skinner played second and I played short. Joe Holland was at third.   In right field was Wood, a son of Mrs. John Wood, that splendid comedienne and a great favorite of the London stage.   Frederick Bond was in left field and Thomas Patten, ex-Postmaster of New York, played center.   We had great fun, and it kept us all in splendid physical shape. When we had no games to play we practiced every morning. We played on tour with local teams. In Chicago, on one trip, we had two fine games—one with the team of the Union Club and the other with a team representing the Board of Trade.

CHAPTER ELEVEN

OF the light comedies produced at Daly's perhaps
the most successful was *A Night Off*. It was
typical of the long line of plays. Daly made this from
the German of Franz and Paul Von Schönthan. The
original of the play was called *Der Raub der Sabin-
erinnen*. We did this play later in London and in
Germany. In New York it was produced early in
March and ran through the rest of the season. It was
revived many times and always seemed uproariously
funny. As a play it was the cleverest and the most
interesting adaptation that Daly made from the
German.

In this play a fly-by-night manager produces a play
written by an old professor. James Lewis was *Professor Babbitt*, and Leclercq was the theatrical manager.
The whole action centers around this play. Miss
Rehan had the ingénue part of *Nisbe;* Mrs. Gilbert
played the wife of the professor. I played *Jack Mulberry*, a younger son of an important English family.
As he could not act he had drifted into this bad
theatrical company. Otis Skinner was *Damask* and

May Irwin was *Susan*, a soubrette. Daly had seen May Irwin at Tony Pastor's. As ever in his career, he liked to find his own people. What went on in other theatres he considered trivial and always of secondary importance to Daly's. He found May Irwin and she joined the company to play this part of *Susan*. She was an extraordinary hit and very funny in a type of soubrette rôle which has almost disappeared from the stage.

On the last night of *A Night Off* a rhymed tag or epilogue, written by Edgar Fawcett, the author of *Our First Families*, which had first served to bring together the four players who were most closely associated with Daly's during the eighties, was read by the actors, each one having a couplet. This ended with some sort of an introduction of Augustin Daly. The manager would then come on and make a speech of acknowledgment for the season which had just passed. This always happened at the end of the season, and Daly never appeared on the first night of a new production or the first night of a season.

Sometimes Fawcett varied this epilogue and one or two of the players would have something a little longer than a distich to recite. On one occasion, to make a rhyme or a quantity correct Fawcett referred to Daly as "the colonel." Daly objected to the rank thus con-

ferred upon him, and Fawcett changed the lines so that
he should be called "the governor." From that time
on we—that is, those of us who were close to the manager—always called Daly, "governor."

It would be difficult to imagine a company in which
there was greater accord than there was at Daly's.
Everything was so fine, and the associations were so
pleasant. No one took offense if the morning greeting
was not as friendly as it should have been; for we were,
in a sense, like a family. Once, playing cricket in
Chicago, I hurt my foot very badly. I spent an evening of torture on the stage trying to disguise my hurt.
Mrs. Gilbert and Miss Rehan were devoted in their
attention during the next few days. Both in and out
of the theatre each had consideration for the others.
Our relations were more than cordial; they were affec-
tionate. We were interested—that is, the so-called Big
Four; we had an interest in the theatre. We were not
partners but every year we received a bonus or a present. I have a gold cigarette case which Daly gave me
one year at the end of the season. Inside was a check
which represented my share of the profits. This semi-
partnership gave us a feeling of responsibility, though
I am unwilling to think that the knowledge of that
bettered our performance.

By the middle eighties first nights at Daly's had

come to be important affairs. As performances they were in no way different from any other performance. Rehearsals were so constant that first nights were as smooth as later ones. But the audiences were very fine and made up of brilliant and prominent people. General Sherman, General Horace Porter, Mark Twain, H. C. Bunner, George William Curtis, Charles Dudley Warner, Frank R. Stockton, Edmund Clarence Stedman, Stanford White, F. D. Millet, Edwin A. Abbey and many others became very closely interested in what went on at Daly's, and they usually tried to be present at the first night of a new play or the revival of an old one.

Mark Twain once wrote the theatre asking that tickets be reserved for him for the first night of a revival. He ended his letter: "I have written wonderful books, which have revolutionized politics and religion in the world; and you might think that this is why my children hold my person to be sacred; but it isn't so; it is because I know Miss Rehan and Mr. Drew personally."

Many critics thought that our best light comedy was *Nancy and Company*. It was a clever adaptation of Rosen's *Halbedichte*, with the scenes and characters transferred to New York. Ada Rehan and I played familiar characters opposite each other.

OTIS SKINNER, EDITH KINGDON, AND JOHN DREW IN
"NANCY AND COMPANY"

In *Love on Crutches* I was *Sidney Austin*, the anonymous writer of a sentimental novel and Ada Rehan was *Annie Austin*, my wife, who is dissatisfied with her home and yearns for a freer existence. She has entered into a correspondence with an author. She does not use her real name. Thus, these two young people who believe themselves unhappily married, conduct a secret correspondence with each other in the belief that they have found their affinities. The happy ending is always in sight. This play, though of little substance, was well acted, and it introduced to Daly audiences Edith Kingdon, the late Mrs. George Gould. As *Margery Gwyn*, she gave a spirited and beautiful comedy performance.

The Railroad of Love, taken from *Goldfische* by Rosen, was a light comedy which may not have been an exact picture of American society, but it was received with enthusiasm and held the stage for some months. Miss Rehan was *Val Osprey* and I was *Lieutenant Howell Everett*. Her part was that of a widow experienced in coquetry. The lieutenant was expert in the subtle arts of the lady-killer.

Edward A. Dithmar writing at the time described the action of this play as follows:

They had met briefly before, but the gentleman did not immediately recognize the lady when they

were introduced at *Mrs. Van Ryker's* ball. She
remembered vividly, however, and could not sup-
press her smiles when she recalled him in the act
of captivating two simple little fräuleins in a
German railway carriage. They flirted, of course.
He employed all his arts, but she outwitted him.
Then chance or Cupid favored him and she was
defeated. It was, at first, a merry war of wit and
mock sentiment, but before two days had passed
they were desperately in love. Then, before they
fully understood each other, that venomous rep-
tile, Jealousy, had crept across their flower-strewn
path, and when it had slinked out of sight again
the woman had written a letter that had to be
recalled before he knew of its existence and she
was at her wit's end to accomplish this purpose.
There was a scene, then, full of passion and emo-
tion, which lifted the comedy far above the level
of frivolous entertainment. The picture of Drew
and Miss Rehan exchanging soft words from
either side of a half-open boudoir door remains
vividly in the memory of folks who saw *The Railroad of Love*, when it was a new play. The scene,
too, in which Drew, as the blind slave of Love,
sat obediently and patiently bending over an em-
broidery frame and bungling the stitches, "one,
two, three, four, cross," was novel and taking.

This play was typical of a long line of plays. And
the description of the action of *The Railroad of Love*,
might almost be substituted for the synopsis of a number of others. The acting and the direction of the
stage made these plays. The success of the Daly

Company was due to these two things rather than to the plays.

But all the adaptations from the German were not so successful as *Needles and Pins*, *A Night Off*, *Nancy and Company*, *The Railroad of Love*, and *Love on Crutches*. *The Passing Regiment* was well played, but the effort to transplant a typically German military story to American soil was not very happy. The visit of a crack militia regiment to a fashionable summer resort was scarcely an equivalent for the quartering of professional soldiers upon the residents of a town by government order. Some of the happenings were as foreign to American soil as anything could be.

Dollars and Sense, *After Business Hours*, *Love in Harness*, *An International Match*, and *The Great Unknown* were all from the German and maintained a fair standard, even if they were not extraordinary successes.

We did, for the first time in America, a number of Pinero's plays: *The Squire*, *Dandy Dick*, *Lords and Commons*—a failure, *The Cabinet Minister* and *The Magistrate*. *The Squire* resembled Hardy's story, "Far From the Madding Crowd." There was a lawsuit over this in England. Pinero insisted that the story had been told him, and that he had not read the Hardy book. Comyns Carr made a dramatization of

Hardy's story and this was done in England and at the Union Square Theatre in New York, where Frederick de Belleville played the leading part. Daly was in no wise involved in this suit. In our version Ada Rehan was *Kate Verity* and I her impetuous lover, *Lieutenant Erick Thorndike*.

In *Dandy Dick* I played the caricature rôle of *Major Tarver*. This play was not a real success, nor was *The Cabinet Minister*. When Ada Rehan heard and read the part that was assigned to her in the latter, she refused to play it. She insisted, and with a great deal of justification, that the leading woman's rôle offered her no opportunities. Isabel Irving played it instead.

When we played *The Magistrate*, Pinero came over to superintend the production. Daly wanted to put Ada Rehan into the part of *Cis Farringdon*, the boy whose mother will not allow him to grow up, as this will fix her own age. Daly thought that because Ada Rehan had made a success as a boy in some of the old comedies she could do this modern boy. Pinero would not have it. He threatened to take his play away from Daly if the latter were to persist in this casting.

Pinero, himself, brought over from London E. Hamilton-Bell to play the boy and he was very good in the part. Bell later designed the costumes for *The Tam-*

JOHN DREW AND ADA REHAN IN "THE SQUIRE," BY
ARTHUR WING PINERO

ing of The Shrew. Ada Rehan played *Mrs. Posket,*
the mother of the boy Daly wanted her to play.

The American production of *The Magistrate* was
not altogether a happy time for Pinero. He did not
like the idea of my playing *Colonel Lukyn,* nor was I
too happy at the prospect of playing the part. The
colonel is a choleric, Anglo-Indian officer. John Clay-
ton had played the character in London, and he was at
that time just what the part called for—a big, stout,
explosive man. For the first time at Daly's I played
an old man. I had to pad, to puff out my cheeks, wear
side whiskers and sparse white hair.

When I came to where Daly and Pinero were standing on the stage at the dress rehearsal I waited for
Daly to offer some criticism of my make-up, but he
merely nodded and walked away.

"Do you think the governor is displeased with my
appearance?" I asked Pinero.

The author was amused at Daly's attitude; he
chuckled a minute and then said: "He merely thinks
that in acquiring a stout old man he has lost a slim
leading man."

On the opening night Pinero was not in the theatre.
He walked around New York until the play was nearly
over. He should have been there to respond to a cur-

tain call at the end of the second act. As he had been nervous about the whole production, he had absented himself and thought that if there would be any demonstration for the author it would be at the end of the play, as is the case in London. When he got to the theatre and saw the people filing out silently he thought the play was a failure.

He came behind the scenes and shook his head; "It didn't go, I suppose?"

We told him that it was a big success and that the play had gone very well. There had been a call for him. We explained that there seldom is any great amount of applause at the end of a play in New York. If a speech is called for from the author it is almost always at the end of the second or third act, as the people here always seem to be in so great a hurry to get out of the building at the end of the play.

The cast for *The Magistrate* was:

MR. POSKET	James Lewis
MR. BULLAMY	Charles Fisher
COL. LUKYN	John Drew
CAPTAIN VALE	Otis Skinner
CIS FARRINGDON	E. Hamilton-Bell
ACHILLE BLOND	Frederick Bond
INSPECTOR MESSITER	Augustus Yorke
AGATHA POSKET	Ada Rehan
CHARLOTTE	Virginia Dreher
BEATIE TOMLINSON	Edith Kingdon
POPHAM	May Irwin

A. M. Palmer, produced a great many plays from the French. Daly in my time in his theatre, found little inspiration in the French authors. We did do Sardou's *Odette*, which was rather grim and somber. It scarcely seemed to fit the Daly repertoire. It was interesting only in that it gave Ada Rehan a chance to do, with great success, an emotional rôle. We also did Sardou's *Golden Widow*, which was called *Marquise* in the original.

I played *Adolphus Doubledot* in *The Lottery of Love*. This play was an adaptation from the French of MM. Bisson, and Mars. Coquelin played it in this country in French with the original title: *Les Surprises du Divorce*. Before his season opened he came to Daly's and saw our version. He congratulated Ada Rehan upon her acting in what was a rather minor rôle, but he said nothing at all to me and I gathered he did not altogether approve of my performance. A short time afterwards he was playing the original play across the street at Palmer's Theatre.

Augustin Daly was fond of the old comedies, and he spent a great deal of time, patience and rehearsal upon these plays. They were not always successful, for the spirit had, in a number of cases, fled long before these revivals. It was quite impossible to breathe life into Farquhar's *The Recruiting Officer*. When Daly did this in February of 1885 it had not been given in New

York for forty-two years. The previous performance was at the old Park Theatre in Park Row. In this production my mother acted *Silvia*, the part played at Daly's by Ada Rehan.

This play is important in the history of New York, for, according to Allston Brown in "A History of the New York Stage," *The Recruiting Officer* was one of the first plays to be given in New York. It was performed as early as 1734, and it had an important production at the first Nassau Street Theatre, September 30, 1750. This was the opening of the season.

Our production was given February 7, 1885, with the parts distributed as follows:

CAPTAIN PLUME	John Drew
CAPT. BRAZEN	George Parkes
JUSTICE BALLANCE	Charles Fisher
SERGEANT KITE	James Lewis
WORTHY	Otis Skinner
BULLOCK	William Gilbert
APPLETREE	Frederick Bond
PEARMAN	Edward Wilks
STEWART	W. H. Beekman
MISTRESS MELINDA	Virginia Dreher
ROSE	May Fielding
LUCY	May Irwin
SYLVIA	Ada Rehan

The revival lasted only about two weeks and then *She Would and She Would Not* was revived. Colley

REHAN AND JOHN DREW IN FARQUHAR'S "THE RECRUITING OFFICER"

Cibber had written this play in imitation of the Span-
ish comedy of intrigue. As was the case with *The
Recruiting Officer*, this play had to be shortened and
edited for use at Daly's. The rôle of *Hypolita*, which
was played by Miss Rehan, and that of *Don Phillip*,
which fell to me, were artificial and by no means easy
to perform. Both of these performances gained in
later years by repetition.

The Country Girl, which was Garrick's adaptation
of Wycherly's *The Country Wife*, was still further
altered so as to include scenes from Congreve's *Love
for Love*. In this Ada Rehan was *Peggy Thrift*, and
I played the leading juvenile, *Belleville*. Ada Rehan's
Peggy was a matchless portrayal. Her success in this
was so great that she kept the play in her repertoire
for many years.

Of course one of the finest of the old comedy productions was *The School for Scandal*. This time Daly
did not make the mistake that he had made at the Fifth
Avenue Theatre. Then he so rearranged Sheridan's
comedy as to destroy the continuity of the scenes. In
his second production the text was altered, but not to
so great an extent. He did, however, change the card
party at *Lady Sneerwell's* to a dance. I had never
played the part of *Charles Surface* before, except
in the screen scene which had been done at a benefit

performance at the Academy of Music in Philadelphia.

The second Daly revival of *The School for Scandal*
was a great success and the cast was:

SIR PETER TEAZLE	Charles Wheatleigh
SIR OLIVER SURFACE	Harry Edwards
SIR BENJ. BACKBITE	Sidney Herbert
SIR HARRY BUMPER	James Macauley
MRS. CANDOUR	Mrs. G. H. Gilbert
LADY SNEERWELL	Adelaide Prince
LADY TEAZLE	Ada Rehan
JOSEPH SURFACE	George Clarke
CHARLES SURFACE	John Drew
CRABTREE	Charles Leclercq
CARELESS	H. Bosworth
MOSES	James Lewis
ROWLEY	John Moore
TRIP	Frederick Bond
SNAKE	Sidney Bowkett
MARIA	Edith Crane

John Ranken Towse, in his "Sixty Years of the
Theatre," has been so gracious as to record: "As
Charles Surface John Drew gave one of the most artistic performances of his career. His impersonation
was second only to that of Charles Coghlan. Especially was it praiseworthy for its artistic restraint in
the drinking scene. He was perhaps a trifle too cool,
insufficiently mercurial for the reckless company he
affected, but he evidently remembered that *Charles*,

with all his follies, was a decent fellow at bottom and not wholly unworthy of the eulogies of his old friend *Rowley*. His manner was elegant, and he spoke his lines without exaggerated emphasis, but with a full appreciation of their humor."

In all these productions of old comedy I had one very great advantage which the other members of the cast did not have. During the rehearsals of one of these plays I always talked over both the play and the part I was to play with my mother. She knew how the characters were to be built up, and their traditions, and she knew the stage business which had been tried and found successful.

CHAPTER TWELVE

Wilt thou have music? hark! Apollo plays
And twenty cagéd nightingales do sing.

THESE words, which were accompanied by a chorus of voices off stage, were my general cue for getting ready—that is, putting on my wig and the final touches of my make-up, before going on to the stage as *Petruchio* in the play proper of *The Taming of the Shrew*. This speech from *The Induction* is in the scene in which the real lord, dressed as a servant, is trying to convince *Sly* that he, one *Christopher Sly*, is really not a tinker, but a lord.

On a night in August of 1888, when I heard these lines, I was leaning out of a window of a turretlike dressing room in the Shakespeare Memorial Theatre at Stratford-on-Avon. It was in the long, English summer twilight and an eight came into sight on the river. As the music which had always been my cue sounded, the coxswain gave the order to cease rowing, and the eight floated past the theatre. The rowers were appreciative listeners to the chorus. They did not

JOHN DREW AS PETRUCHIO IN "THE TAMING OF THE SHREW"

know that an American company was playing *The Taming of the Shrew* in Shakespeare's home town.

Actually, the performance that night was no different from the one we ordinarily gave, but I think it was the most picturesque night I have ever spent in the theatre.

The house bill announced that at The Memorial Theatre, Friday, August 3, 1888, Mr. Augustin Daly's company of American Comedians would give for the benefit of the memorial library fund Shakespeare's comedy *The Taming of the Shrew*, as presented by them for one hundred twenty-five nights in New York and lately played with great success at The Gaiety Theatre, London. The bill went on to add: "This comedy, as presented by Mr. Daly's Company, will be performed for the first time in Stratford-on-Avon, and the proceeds will be generously devoted to the Library Fund of the Shakespeare Memorial."

Earlier that day we had gone to Stratford. We were personally conducted by William Winter, who was always at the Daly parties in New York or London, and on special trips like this he invariably accompanied us. As he had written books about the Shakespeare country, he was the acknowledged head of the expedition and in front of the Shakespeare house he made a speech. We were quite a crowd, for in addi-

Memorial Theatre, Stratford=on=Avon,

Friday Evening, August 3rd, 1888,

AT 7.30,

AUGUSTIN DALY'S COMPANY OF COMEDIANS

IN SHAKESPEARE'S COMEDY,

The Taming of the Shrew,

(Prepared for the occasion by AUGUSTIN DALY).

●●●●●●●●●●●●●●●●●●●●●●●●●●●●●●

Characters in the "Induction."

A Lord	.. Mr. GEORGE CLARKE
Christopher Sly........................ *A drunken Tinker*...............	Mr. WILLIAM GILBERT
A Huntsman	...Mr. EUGENE ORMOND
The Hostess	Miss LIZZIE St. QUENTIN
A Page .... *Representing a Lady*...............	Master W. COLLIER
Huntsmen	Messrs. REVELL, MURPHY, and FINNEY
Players	Messrs. BOND and WOOD

Persons in the Comedy.

Baptista ....*A rich gentleman of Padua*............	Mr. CHARLES FISHER
Vincentio ....*An old gentleman of Pisa*....................	Mr. JOHN MOORE
Lucentio ....*Son to Vincentio, loving Bianca*............	Mr. OTIS SKINNER
Petrucio ... .*A gentleman of Verona, suitor to Katherine*.........Mr. JOHN DREW
Gremio ....*An old gentleman* { *Suitors to* } ...Mr. CHARLES LECLERQ
Hortensio .... *A young gentleman* { *Bianca* } ... Mr. JOSEPH HOLLAND
A Pedant............ ......*An old fellow, set up to represent Vincentio*.........Mr. JOHN WOOD
Grumio ... .Serving man to Petrucio................ Mr. JAMES LEWIS
Biondello ....} *Servants to Lucentio* { ....Mr. E. P. WILKS
Tranio ....} { .... Mr. FREDERICK BOND
Guests, &c., by Misses Campbell, Sears, Conron, Vislairo, Ferrell, Cooke, &c.
Katherine ....*The Shrew*.......................... Miss ADA REHAN
Bianca ....*Her Sister* .... Miss PHŒBE RUSSELL
A Widow...........................*Who marries Hortensio* .... Miss ALICE HOOD
Curtis ....*Of Petrucio's household*.................Mrs. G. H. GILBERT

AUGUSTIN DALY'S MOST FAMOUS PRODUCTION

tion to the entire cast for a big Shakespearian production there were Daly, his wife and his brother; William Winter; an American playwright, Henry Dam; the attendant stage people and all the London correspondents of the American newspapers.

In front of the Shakespeare House, just as Winter was making his speech, two natives were attracted to this unusually large crowd, thinking that something had happened, that someone had dropped dead or had had a fit. They listened a minute to Winter.

"Aw, come on, Bill," said one of them; "it's the same old game."

They had seen American tourists before, and on the rest of our long walk to Anne Hathaway's cottage we attracted little attention.

In the afternoon we rowed on the river. Daly, who always stage-managed things, even to the seats the minor people were to occupy on trains, arranged us in boats. Otis Skinner and I rowed the boat in which Daly and Mrs. Daly and Ada Rehan were seated. At one point one of the other boats threatened us. As it was part of Daly's scheme that he should be first, we were urged to new effort and were soon in the lead.

During our stay in Stratford we stopped at the Red Lion Inn. On the night of our arrival we dined at Clopton Hall, the residence of Sir Arthur Hodgson, the mayor of Stratford. *The Lord* of *The Induction* of *The Taming of the Shrew* is supposed to be the *Baron Clopton* of Shakespeare's time, and the hall where the play is supposed to be given before *Christopher Sly*, the hall in which we were now entertained. The next day we had luncheon at Avonbank, the residence of Charles Flower, and Robert Laffan, the headmaster of the King Edward VI Grammar School, entertained us at tea.

The attention that we received on this visit to Stratford was very different from the reception that we got on our unheralded first visit to London in the summer of 1884. Then the social season was over, and we were really too late to do well. We played in a little theatre, Toole's, in King William Street, just off the Strand.

Before our opening Jim Lewis and I went to see Charles Wyndham and Mary Moore at the Criterion. This graceful comedian, who had been a surgeon in the American Civil War and was always a great favorite in this country, was playing one of those delightfully done English comedies that he and Mary Moore did for so many years.

Lewis and I came away from this performance gloomily. We did not think that our company could succeed where people were accustomed to such work as Wyndham and his associates were giving. We opened in *7–20–8*, one of our numerous plays from the German. We were required in London to call this play by its subtitle, *Casting a Boomerang*. Yorke Stephens had copyrighted a play from the German original and had used the title *7–20–8*. We did *Dollars and Sense*, also a modern play; but our greatest success was won with the old comedy, *She Would and She-Would Not*. After our London engagement we returned to New York. The venture was not signally successful, nor yet so discouraging as to prevent our returning.

The second visit to London was in May, 1886. This time the season was right. The company opened in *A Night Off*. "It was a greeting to dear old friends, and in spirit at least there was a hearty shaking of hands across the footlights, with Mr. Lewis and Mrs. Gilbert, Mr. Drew and Miss Rehan, Mr. Skinner and Miss Dreher and their clever companions," observed *The Era*. The same paper also said: "Nowhere is greater regard paid to the sex, and this, of course, is reflected upon the stage. There women are placed on a nearly equal status with men, in personal liberty, in intellectual attainments; comedy is likely to flourish;

and if the comedy of America has hardly as yet taken the highest place, there is little doubt as to its ultimate development, influence and power."

Of our performance in *Nancy and Company*, which followed, the *Saturday Review* said: "There is not now in London, an English company as well chosen, as well trained, as brilliant in the abilities of its individual members, or as well harmonized as a whole, as the admirable company which Mr. Daly directs. They suggest the Comédie Française at its very best, when it is not frozen stiff by its own chill dignity. Every performance shows that they are controlled by a single mind strong in the knowledge of its own aim and ability."

Of course by this time we were very successful and had acquired a tremendous following. We were talked of and asked about a great deal. At a reception a woman asked me: "Have you seen the *Dalys?*"

I said: "Oh, yes, I glanced over *The Post* and *The Telegraph.*"

"Oh, no," she protested, "I mean the Dalys." Then she recognized me as one of the players.

Henry Labouchère, that great journalist and editor, wrote in *Truth:* "When Daly first came to England, the company was pronounced by our theatrical guides, philosophers and friends as a complete failure. At

JOHN DREW, MRS. GILBERT, AND JAMES LEWIS, IN "7–20–8," THE FIRST
PLAY DONE BY AUGUSTIN DALY'S COMPANY IN LONDON

present, although the company is the same and the plays are the same, everything is declared to be perfection."

Royalty attended our performances, and one night, when we were playing at the Gaiety Theatre, the Prince of Wales, later Edward VII, asked Ada Rehan and myself to come into his box. With him was his wife, now the dowager Queen Alexandra, and a young relation of hers from Denmark. The Prince of Wales was very affable, but he rather ignored Daly who ushered us into the box. In the managerial department of the London theatres everyone wore dinner clothes. Daly never dressed for the theatre.

The Prince of Wales asked us whether or not Shakespeare was popular in America. He had seen the advance billing that we were to do *The Taming of the Shrew*. The play that night was *Love on Crutches*, and he did not seem to care for it. This play never did go so well in London as it had in New York.

When we got back to the stage some of the other players crowded round us. They wanted to know about our reception.

"Who was the other man in the box?" asked Leclercq.

"He is one of the Princes of Denmark. The Princess of Wales is his aunt," I explained.

"What's he doing over here?"

"I don't know. They did not let us in on the purpose of his mission."

"I know what he's doing here," said Jim Lewis; "he has come over here from Denmark to collect royalties from Henry Irving for *Hamlet*."

CHAPTER THIRTEEN

ON our trip abroad in 1886, we went to Germany and played in Hamburg and Berlin. This was the first and only time that an entire American company visited Germany. This jaunt, which Daly undertook as an advertisement of the company, was really a greater success than might have been supposed. Of course, in neither German city were they particularly pleased with the adapted version of their own plays, played by an English-speaking company. The writers of these plays were extremely glad to see us, as they had made a good thing out of the Daly adaptations and, because of the higher royalties paid, they made more money out of the American rights.

In Hamburg six plays were given: *Love on Crutches*, *A Night Off*, *Nancy and Company*, *A Woman's Won't*, *The Country Girl* and *She Would and She Would Not*. For the two English plays, *The Country Girl* and *She Would and She Would Not* full arguments were printed in the program. It was taken for granted that the German farces would be familiar, and merely the title and author of the German plays

whole theatre was extremely well ordered. Maids were provided for the women, and dressers for the men. The dressers, who were really tailor's helpers or bushelmen, were very efficient.

The dresser who looked after me was so zealous in the performance of his job that he followed me onto the stage one night. In *Love on Crutches* there was a scene in the last act in which Lewis and I stood at the back of the stage, partly concealed from the audience. Mrs. Gilbert and William Gilbert (he was no relation whatever) were playing a scene that was full of laughs before an American audience.

On this night before a German audience it was going very badly. Lewis whispered to me: "I'll bet you that Grandma gets the first laugh."

Before I could answer him I got the first laugh, for just then my dresser, who had followed me down from the dressing room, pulled up my coat at the neck. He had not been quite satisfied with the way the coat set and righted it in full view of the audience.

After the performance we went to a garden where we could get something to eat and listen to some music. Jim Lewis and Mrs. Lewis, May Irwin, Otis Skinner and I sat there under the trees for some time. When it came time to pay our checks, Lewis insisted that he would pay. He suddenly discovered that he had no

EDITH KINGDON (GOULD) AS SHE APPEARED WITH THE DALY COMPANY

money. He had taken the precaution to change his money to his stage clothes early in the evening, but had not remembered to put it back. He decided to get it now. We were to wait for him.

We sat there for an interminable time, and then, as Mrs. Lewis was worried about him, we went out to look for him. We found him only about two houses away leaning against the wall. He was exhausted; he had been wandering about everywhere.

I asked him: "Did you find your wad?"

"Find it! I couldn't find the theatre," he said in an injured manner. "I met several policemen and they affected not to understand me."

"What did you ask them?"

"Why for the 'Wolmar' Theater of course."

"If you pronounced it that way, it is no wonder they couldn't direct you to the theatre," both Skinner and I protested.

Lewis was never convinced that there was any reason for his not getting his money till the next day except a willful failure to understand him on the part of the police.

Our happy relations were somewhat strained in Berlin by the abrupt departure from the company of Edith Kingdon. Just before we left London she had been called upon with almost no notice to play Ada Rehan's

Burnand replied: "Yes, and they don't get in."

Grossmith answered: "I don't know who it is who sends the good things to *Punch*, but they don't get in."

This created a great laugh at Burnand's expense.

Tennyson I met at his place in the country, and he talked to me of the play that he was then writing, *The Foresters*. We did this play later at Daly's Theatre; in fact, the part of *Robin Hood* in this was the last new part I played under the management of Augustin Daly. I was no longer a member of the Daly company when the play was done by them in London. Arthur Bouchier took my part. *The Foresters* was never a great success. By reason of Arthur Sullivan's music and Daly's production, the play managed to run for a time in New York.

Swinburne and Hardy were at many of the dinners and suppers that we attended in London, and Hardy wrote a very charming rhymed address that Ada Rehan read at a benefit for the Actors' Dramatic Fund.

Meredith I met once in the country. He was staying with a friend near where we were at Weybridge in Surrey, and we went over to see him.

Some of the other guests danced in bare feet on the lawn.

I asked Meredith if he were not going to dance.

man repertoire" and then had the "effrontery" to put his own name on the work. M. Besson, of *L'Evènement*, thought that the repertoire was "fit only for boarding schools," and M. Sarcey, the leading critic of the day, wrote that the plays might be seen by "any young girl." These opinions are interesting because some of the critics thought the plays too realistic, coarse and offensive.

Not all of the criticism was adverse and hostile. Some of the critics were sympathetic. M. de Blowitz, the correspondent of the *London Times* in Paris, wrote in correspondence to his paper that the failure of the Daly Company to win the praise of the critics in Paris was due to the fact that the French writers did not know English, and that those Frenchmen who understood the language appreciated the fine acting of the company in light comedy.

It was very hot in Paris that summer, and the time we were not rehearsing or playing, Otis Skinner and I spent at a swimming bath on the other side of the Seine. The place was inclosed, but open to the sky. There were dressing rooms all round the sides. We occasioned much talk by going up on top of these and diving into the water. It was not really high, but the other bathers seemed to think it foolhardy and dangerous.

JOHN DREW AND VIRGINIA DREHER IN "THE COUNTRY GIRL"

Our last night at the theatre was crowded with excitement. The gas was turned off in the dressing rooms before some of us had time to wash off our make-up. I lost my trunk. The concierge, feeling that he had not received a sufficient tip from Daly, waged a most fearful quarrel with him. The manager was accused among other things of having taken three towels that belonged to the theatre.

While I was having my own battle with the man I had seen take my trunk—and he professed to know nothing about it—I could hear part of this larger engagement.

"What's he saying now?" Daly, who spoke no French, would demand of his interpreter.

"Oh, I can't tell you. I can't tell you," the interpreter would answer every few seconds.

The next day, before we left town, I went back to the theatre again and there was my trunk in a conspicuous place where I could not have failed to see it, had it been there the night before. I put it on my cab without the help of any of the theatre people and drove off amid their imprecations and anathemas.

Two years later, when the Daly Company again played the same theatre, the same stage-door keeper greeted me as an old acquaintance. This second visit to Paris was a far happier experience for the Daly

Company. This time we gave three plays during an engagement that lasted six days: *Nancy and Company*, *The Railroad of Love* and *The Taming of the Shrew*.

The critics devoted their attention to Shakespeare. A writer in *Le Petit Journal* exclaimed: "Pauvre Shakespeare! What crimes are committed in thy name, and how fortunate that thou hast been dead some time!" M. Sarcey found the comedy illogical. He could see no fun in one character hitting another with a leg of mutton. When I read this criticism to Daly, he was amused and, though he knew no French, he at once called attention to Molière's *Le Marriage Forcé*, in which stuffed rocks and clubs are plied with great advantage on the classic French stage.

Many of the critics thought there was too much horse play; they were shocked when *Katherine* boxed *Petruchio's* ears. They found too much violence in the playing. Then, too, the play was coarse and flat and dull.

Figaro, which discovered that I resembled Irving, said: "The attitudes, movements, walk, speech and action of these Americans are so different from what we are accustomed to see and hear that there would be neither justice nor profit in criticising them. It is another race, another conception, another art. "

CHAPTER SIXTEEN

VERY different had been the reception given to *The Taming of the Shrew* when we gave it earlier that same summer in London. This was the first performance of a Shakespearian play given by an American Company in Europe. The *Times* said that till this Daly production, it seemed that this comedy was "fated to rank as the most despised of the poet's productions," and that hitherto the play had "received scant justice from the professional interpreters—so at least it would appear—in view of this splendid revival of the comedy, which, sumptuously mounted and acted with admirable spirit and point, keeps the house throughout its five acts in a state of continuous merriment."

The summer that we were playing *The Taming of the Shrew* in London, I was going down to Sandown to see the Eclipse Stakes—that was the year that Bendigo won—and at Waterloo Station my companion bought a copy of *Punch*.

He opened it, laughed and handed the paper to me. "Look at that," he said.

It was a cartoon showing Mr. and Mrs. Kendal looking out of a box in the theatre and in the box on the opposite side were the Bancrofts. On the stage were Ada Rehan as *Katherine* and myself as *Petruchio*. We were depicted in the clothes worn in the scene in which *Petruchio* dresses fantastically. I was supposed to be saying to these representatives of the English stage who were seated in the boxes: "I guess we'll show you how to play your gosh-dinged Shakespeare."

The year that Ormonde won the Derby, Daly hired a four-in-hand and we drove down to Epsom. Daly had wanted to have a matinee that day, but William Terriss, who was associated with Daly in our first two trips abroad, refused to have a performance on the ground that nobody would be in town.

Daly somewhat reluctantly consented to go to the races, in which he was not much interested, and Terriss accompanied us. Following his usual custom Daly arranged the seating on the drag and reserved the box seat with the driver for himself.

"You can't do that," I protested.

"Why not?" he asked.

"It just isn't done," I told him; "a woman is always on the box seat next to the driver."

With very bad grace he yielded the seat he had chosen for himself to Ada Rehan.

CARTOON FROM PUNCH

We saw one of the greatest Derbys that had been run for many years. Ormonde, owned by the Duke of Westminster, was a great horse. He was ridden by Fred Archer, the leading English jockey. Ormonde was later sold and sent to the Argentine, and he was eventually bought by my old friend, William McDonough, of California. Years after his Epsom victory I saw Ormonde in the stud at McDonough's ranch.

In London I met some of the American artists and writers that I had not met in this country—Sargent, Henry James and Bret Harte. The first time that I met Bret Harte was the Fourth of July, 1888. He had been United States consul in Glasgow and was at the time I met him living in London.

That summer there was a cyclorama in London that was very popular, called *Niagara in London*. It was the usual entertainment in the conventional round building that somewhat resembled the outside of Shakespeare's Theatre, the Globe. The management, being partly American and Canadian, gave a supper in the cyclorama building on the night of the Fourth. Bret Harte, Edward Phelps, who was then our minister to England, and many prominent Americans were there.

While we walked around and looked at this constructed picture of Niagara, which was not so wonderful to us as to the Englishmen present, Lewis and I talked to Bret Harte. He was a very handsome man, and he impressed us very much, though his manner was quite casual.

After the two national anthems were sung, the supper room opened and the people flocked in and found seats for themselves. Lewis and I were sitting next to an Englishman, who was evidently very hungry and very thirsty. Mr. Phelps, the American minister, walked into the room and looked about, over the tables. He wore side whiskers and to a chance observer looked not unlike a maître d'hôtel. The Englishman, not knowing who it was, mistook him for one of the waiters and asked him to bring him a bottle of Apollinaris. He pointed to a bottle near by that had been opened.

Phelps very goodnaturedly took the bottle and put it down in front of the Englishman and started to walk away.

The Englishman was very irate because Phelps had not filled the glass. He reprimanded him and, as he did so, he stood up and called to the retreating figure: "What do you mean by this? And who are you?"

Phelps turned and answered: "My name is Phelps. I am the American minister at the court of St. James's."

The Englishman fell back in his chair so violently that he knocked the chair over backwards.

"Did you get his back-fall?" Lewis asked of me.

In theatrical parlance a "back-fall" is a comic flop or fall on the stage. It is an old-fashioned, low-comedy method of denoting terror or fright.

CHAPTER SEVENTEEN

THE most brilliant entertainment given for us during our many stays in London was the supper which John Hare gave at the Garrick Club on June 9, 1888. It was a wonderful list of guests and contained almost everyone prominent in the arts—actors, authors, painters, managers—Millais, Henry James, Du Maurier, Ambassador Phelps and the Earls of Lathorn, Londesborough and Cork and Orrery were all present.

For some reason, known only to himself, Daly absented himself from this supper. It was believed that he was annoyed that Hare had not submitted to him the list of those members of the Daly Company who were to be asked. Irving was furious at Daly, and so was William Winter, who was one of Daly's closest friends.

When John Hare made a speech, I had to respond in place of Daly. I was not very happy, and I was a little upset because Hare had used a few of the things that I was going to say. I was so disturbed that at one portion of my speech I halted like an actor who forgets his lines. I do not know what happened to me or what caused the sudden lapse, but I could not preserve the continuity of the thing. I knew it was very bad.

When I had finished Sir Arthur Sullivan, who was sitting a few seats away from me, came over and shook me by the hand and said: "It was fine. Capital!"

Lord Cork, who was sitting just beyond Sullivan, also said: "Capital! Capital!"

I thought it was very good of them, but it did not deceive me. It took me a long time to recover from my embarrassment.

Charles Wyndham gave a garden party one Sunday. That year he had Pope's famous villa at Twickenham on the Thames. Lewis, Ada Rehan, Mrs. Gilbert, Daly and I went down. It rained all day, and we were rather cooped up in the tents where the refreshments were served.

While the band was playing Wyndham took hold of his sister, who was the wife of Bronson Howard, the American author of Wyndham's successful play *Brighton* (*Saratoga* in this country), and rushed her out on the fearfully wet lawn and danced around a few times. He was determined that there should be dancing at his party. He put up an umbrella, and it looked so ridiculous to see him waltzing around on the wet lawn one arm holding up the umbrella and the other arm around his sister.

During the run of *The Taming of the Shrew* we were asked to play for a dramatic fund benefit at the Drury Lane Theatre. We played the fourth act of *The Taming of the Shrew*—the scene in which *Petruchio* trying to frighten and impress *Katherine* with his masterfulness, whacks his servants about the stage with his whip and a "property" leg of mutton. His servants were played by Lewis as *Grumio*, William Collier, Hamilton Revelle and Stephen Murphy, who afterwards took the name of Stephen Grattan when he went to the Lyceum Theatre in New York. Murphy had a pedantic fashion of speaking, and he took himself and his work very seriously.

In this fourth-act scene the servants are intensely surprised at *Petruchio's* behavior toward them, as they had known him always as a kindly master. When *Petruchio* and *Katherine* exit, the servant played by Stephen Murphy has to say: "Peter, didst ever see the like?" referring to Petruchio's extraordinary behavior.

Murphy was much impressed with the fact that he was about to utter something of the immortal bard in the famous Drury Lane Theatre where Garrick, Macready and Kemble had played. At the rehearsal he said to Collier in an awed voice: "Collier, do you

From Theatre Collection, Harvard University.

FROM LEFT TO RIGHT: JOHN DREW, JAMES LEWIS, ADA REHAN, CHARLES FISHER, VIRGINIA DREHER, MRS. G. H. GILBERT, OTIS SKINNER, AND MAY IRWIN, IN "A NIGHT OFF"

realize that I am to have the precious privilege of speaking a line of Shakespeare in this sacred fane?"

Collier interrupted with, "What's a fane?"

Murphy, impatient at the interruption, replied: "Fane? A fane is a convertible term for temple. It is a temple."

"Oh, yes," said Collier, apparently entirely satisfied with the definition.

When, in the actual playing of the scene, the cue came for Murphy's great moment Collier came in quickly on the cue and spoke the line: "Peter, didst ever see the like?" before the outraged Murphy had a chance to do so.

Collier sensed from Murphy's expression of disappointment and anger that there would be trouble. Indeed, as soon as the scene was over Murphy made a dash for Collier. Collier, being more agile, avoided the rush and was chased all over the stage behind the scenes by Murphy.

I demanded to know from these two fellows what caused the horrible commotion while Ada Rehan and I were playing the last scene. Murphy told me that Collier had deliberately tried to belittle him; that he had robbed him of his great opportunity to read a line of Shakespeare in Drury Lane and go down into theatrical history with the Keans, Kembles and Garrick.

CHAPTER EIGHTEEN

THE years that we did not go to London the Daly Company made a tour to the Pacific Coast. In the lobby of the Baldwin Hotel in San Francisco Jim Lewis and I one summer day met Sir Arthur Sullivan, the composer. We had met him often in London. When we saw him this day he had arrived from Australia; in fact he was just off the boat. He greeted us most effusively, for he had been living for some months in a country where he knew no one. He introduced us to the man who was with him, the captain of the steamer that had brought him to California.

Then, after a few minutes' conversation, he again shook hands warmly and said: "We are going to have a drink. Good-by."

I was amused, but Lewis was intensely annoyed at the casualness of Sullivan's remark. He said: "I wouldn't have accepted it, but he might have asked us."

As a matter of fact, Lewis never did drink in the daytime. While I was laughing at Lewis' annoyance, we were joined by that great favorite of the road, Sol Smith Russell. His *Hosea Howe* in *Peaceful Valley* and his *Noah Vale* in *The Poor Relation* were only a little less well known than Jefferson's *Rip*.

Russell was one of those long-looking persons, and he had an extraordinary manner of dressing. He always wore a black frock coat and a little white string tie. He looked much like a minister, and he told me that when he was purchasing things in shops he was often offered the clerical discount.

When he joined us that morning in San Francisco he was on his way to the dentist's. He urged me to go with him. As I had nothing to do I thought I would walk with him a while. We soon reached the place of his appointment, and he persuaded me to go in and wait for him.

In the dentist's waiting room was an old lady who was apparently in great pain. She was bewailing her condition. She looked at Russell and, thinking to get some spiritual advice, said to him: "Are you a minister?"

Russell answered, paraphrasing from *Macbeth:* "I minister to minds diseased."

"No," she said, "are you a real minister?"

Russell answered: "No, madam, I am only a poor player."

She then asked: "A piano player?"

It was so absurd and I laughed so loudly that the

old woman was much incensed. She seemed to think that a dentist's waiting room was no place to laugh. Russell had persuaded me to accompany him to sustain him morally, and spiritual advice was demanded from him!

As the Daly Company toured the various cities of the country we were much entertained. Sometimes entertainment was thrust upon us when we thought we were in a town where no one knew us.

Otis Skinner and I, on our way from the theatre to our hotel in one of the smaller cities of the Middle West, stepped into a small vaudeville theatre which kept open till midnight. We wanted to stand up at the rear of the theatre, but we were not allowed to do so. We were spotted at once and ushered by the management to seats in the very front of the theatre.

As we took our seats someone was clattering away on the stage with a noisy song and clog dance. We noticed that the door under the stage was opened and a man stuck his head out and handed something written on a paper to one of the musicians, who in turn handed it to the leader.

The next act was a singer, known in the nineties as a motto singer. I remember nothing about him except that he pointed to Skinner and myself and sang a song about the poor actor in distress. I do not know this

GEORGIE DREW BARRYMORE WITH ETHEL, LIONEL, AND JACK
BARRYMORE

song, and I do not know whether it ever went the
rounds of the popular theatres. When he reached the
end he came and stood directly in front of Skinner
and myself and sang words which ran something like
this:

> Do all you can for the actor in distress;
>   Engage him before it's too late;
> For many a poor actor can give a good show,
>   So give the poor actor a date.

At the height of the fame of the Daly Company—
and this was after we had produced many notable successes—we were booked as the opening attraction of
a new theatre in Rockford, Illinois. The theatre was
a very fine one, and the occasion an important one lo-
cally. After the first performance, which was somewhat delayed by speech making and special ceremonies,
Jim Lewis and I were sitting in the lobby of the hotel.

A man kept walking up and down in front of us,
and it seemed quite obvious that he wanted to talk.
After running his fingers through his beard in the manner of a stage rustic, he cleared his throat and stopped
short in front of us; "I seen you act tonight," he said.

"I trust you were edified," said Lewis.

The native laughed, as if appreciating a huge joke.
"I dunno about that; I thought it was pretty good.
You folks ought to stay here some time. I hear most

of the reserved seats is bought up for tomorrow night." He dropped into the arm chair next to Lewis and continued: "I talked to the manager of the theatre tonight, and we come to the conclusion that yours is the best trained troupe that has ever been here since *Humpty-Dinky*."

It is needless to say that he referred to the ever popular pantomime performance *Humpty-Dumpty*, which toured the country for years.

Lewis groaned, and I thought things. This was praise indeed! The Daly Company was supposed to be the best in the country. We had been allowed to believe by the press and the public that we were the best exponents of light-comedy acting. Our acting was supposed to be most finished. We had been received in London as perhaps no foreign company ever has been. We had played in France and Germany. We had been made much of by many important people. Enthusiasts had compared our company with the Comédie Française.

I do not believe that either Lewis or I heard any of the rest of the conversation of our newly acquired friend.

CHAPTER NINETEEN

DURING a lunch at Delmonico's early in the winter of 1888 the talk shifted occasionally from the subject we had met to discuss and Mark Twain told a story in his inimitable way. I do not remember what the story itself was but while we were all laughing, General Sherman said: "That story lost nothing in the telling, Clemens."

"I didn't mean that it should," replied the teller of the story.

Edwin Booth, Lawrence Hutton, A. M. Palmer, Harry Edwards, Stephen Olin, Thomas Bailey Aldrich, Lawrence Barrett, Augustin Daly, William Bispham, Joseph F. Daly, Samuel Clemens, General Sherman, James Lewis and I were sitting round the table.

The reason for gathering together these men representing the professions was to discuss the founding of The Players. The idea to have a club where the persons of the several arts could meet had been discussed by Booth, Barrett, Hutton and others on Commodore Benedict's yacht, *The Oneida*.

After lunch a number of us went down to 16 Gramercy Park to look over the site which had been chosen for The Club.

On New Year's Eve, 1888, The Players was formally opened. It was founded entirely through the generosity of Edwin Booth. He was the first President and upon his death in 1893 Joseph Jefferson became the second. Upon the death of the latter the honor was conferred upon me, and ever since I have held the office so splendidly filled by those two great men of the profession.

As to the ideal and the purpose of this splendid gift to the members of the acting profession, nothing can be better said than it is in those words that Edwin Booth used in his speech of dedication:

Gentlemen: Although our vocations are various, I greet you all as brother Players. At this supreme moment of my life, it is my happy privilege to assume the character of host, to welcome you to the house wherein I hope that we for many years, and our legitimate successors for at least a thousand generations, may assemble for friendly intercourse and intellectual recreation. Especially for the worthy ones of my profession am I desirous that this association shall be the means of bringing them, regardless of their theatrical rank, in communion with those who, ignorant of their personal qualities hidden by the mask and motley of our calling, know them as actors only.

Frequent intercourse with gentlemen of other arts and professions, who love the stage and appreciate the value of the drama as an aid to intellectual culture, must inspire the humblest player with a reverence for his vocation as one among the first of "fine arts"—which too many regard as merely a means to the gratification of vanity and selfishness. Such is the object of this club.

For many years I have cherished the hope that I might be able to do something for my profession of a more lasting good than mere almsgiving, but could not determine what course to pursue. Our several benevolent institutions for the relief of poor and disabled actors (foremost among them the noble Forrest Home), great as their good work is, do not afford the social advantages so necessary for what is termed "the elevation of the stage."

Not until after many conversations with numerous friends of the theatre on this subject, and while discussing it with Messrs. Barrett, Daly, and Palmer (a club of this character being suggested as the best means to the good end), did I resolve to act, to do my utmost in the furtherance of the scheme proposed. This is the first step toward the accomplishment of our purpose. To our treasurer, Mr. William Bispham, we owe the wise selection of our house, to Mr. Stanford White its admirable reconstruction and embellishment, while to the poet Aldrich we are indebted for the choice of our appropriate and comprehensive title, the world being but a stage where every man must "play his part." Mine just now, as the New Year dawns, is a very happy one, since it permits me to present to you by the hands of our vice-president, Mr. Daly, your title deeds to this property.

Having done so, I am no longer your host—I resign the rôle with profound thanks for your prompt and generous cooperation in a cause so dear to me, so worthy of all well-wishers of the theatre and of the Player who "struts and frets his hour upon the stage."

Let us drink from this loving-cup, bequeathed by William Warren of loved and honored memory to our no less valued Jefferson, and by him presented to us—from this cup and this souvenir of long ago, my father's flagon, let us now, beneath his portrait, and on the anniversaries of this occupation, drink: "To the Players' Perpetual Prosperity!"

CHAPTER TWENTY

I WAS still playing at Daly's theatre when I first met Charles Frohman. He then had the Twenty-third Street Theatre, now Proctor's, and had produced Bronson Howard's famous drama of the Civil War, *Shenandoah*, which had so much to do with the founding of his theatrical fortune.

In the men's café at Delmonico's, then at Broadway and Twenty-sixth Street, I often saw a little round man who I thought was Alfred Klein, the brother of Charles Klein, the author of *The Music Master* and *The Lion and the Mouse*. Alfred Klein, was one of three brothers connected with the theatre. He played with Gillette in *The Professor*, and some years afterwards he was the elephant trainer with DeWolf Hopper in *Wang*.

Anson Pond, the writer of a play called *Her Atonement*, protested to me one day: "Why, that's not Klein. That is Charles Frohman, the coming theatrical manager."

At that time I was not much interested in other theatrical managers. Ada Rehan, Lewis and the rest of us at Daly's felt that these newer managers were intruders. Daly never thought what happened outside of his theatre was of any importance, and this spirit of his prejudiced us.

One fine Sunday Fritz Williams and I rode out to Claremont. Seated at a table near us was Frank Sanger and the man I had mistaken for Alfred Klein. I had known Frank Sanger in Philadelphia. He had been one of the players, though not a conspicuous one, in the stock company at the Chestnut Street Theatre. He became night clerk in the Hotel La Pierre one summer. Later he got into theatrical management and made a great deal of money out of Charles Hoyt's play, *A Bunch of Keys*. With Hayman he built the Empire Theatre for Charles Frohman.

At this meeting at Claremont Sanger and Frohman joined us. Sanger turned the conversation, in a rather diplomatic fashion, to the possibilities of my changing managements. I do not mean to imply that this conversation was exactly prearranged.

Sanger said: "John is wedded to Daly as a manager."

"I don't know about that," I answered.

"You're not thinking of changing, are you?" Sanger asked.

"No," I told him; "but I'm not bound as a serf."

MAUDE ADAMS AND JOHN DREW IN HENRY GUY CARLETON'S PLAY, "BUTTERFLIES"

One Sunday evening Henry Miller took me to Frohman's apartment in the Hoffman House to play cards. Miller and I met Frohman and Anson Pond, who was a great friend of his, in the lobby of the hotel. We played poker for a while, and I felt, as subsequent events developed, that I had been allowed to win and had not won through my own cleverness or prowess with the cards. I do not know whether I was right about this, but I do know that Frohman was a very good card player, as was Pond. We had a very elaborate "terrapinish" supper and went back to card playing.

Conversations with Sanger, which were usually predicated upon the supposition of what I would do if I left Daly, and occasional meetings with Frohman went on for some time. Finally an offer came through Frank Bennett, who was manager of the old Arlington Hotel in Washington.

Frank Bennett, who was the son-in-law of my godmother, Mrs. D. P. Bowers, had been an actor for a time in the Daly company, but he became discouraged and gave up the stage. Fortunately for him he had the keenness of perception, given to very few people who want to act, to realize that there was no future for him. On one of our trips with the Daly company to Washington he met Roselle, proprietor of the Arlington Hotel, who offered him a job.   From this he rose to be manager.

"Why don't you get out of your engagement with Daly, John?" Bennett asked me on one occasion.   I suppose my manner seemed receptive to him, for he went on: "Frohman is the coming man."

Frohman apparently had calculated that I had a drawing power, and in this he seems to have had faith, for a most generous offer was made to me by Bennett. I authorized him to make a suggestion or two to Frohman and the thing was accomplished.

At the time there was still more than a year of my contract with Daly to run.   I told Daly at once that I was leaving him at the end of our arrangement.   I felt that I was at liberty to go and that there was no moral obligation upon my part to stay with a manager with whom I had been for so many seasons.   I felt this because Daly had before this rescinded the agreement that he had with Mrs. Gilbert, Miss Rehan, Lewis and myself.   He had given us a share in the profits of the season apart from our salaries.   It was a semi-proprietary arrangement similar to that enjoyed by the actors at the Comédie Française, that is, the Societaires who have all had certain years of service.

Daly wrote us that "in view of certain contingencies" he had decided that it was inexpedient to continue this arrangement. He proposed that we take increased salaries in place of the percentage. A small increase in salary went into effect, but a season or two afterwards, when I asked Daly for more money, he declined to give it to me.

Frohman offered me a salary much larger than Daly ever contemplated giving anyone connected with his theatre. Accordingly, I signed my first contract with Frohman. It was for three years; I never had another. We merely went on from year to year. During our whole professional business associations there was never a difference of any sort. I received a salary and at the end of the season a percentage of the year's receipts.

Once, when I thought I should have a larger salary, I went to Charles Frohman and told him so. "Charles, I spoke to you several years ago about giving me more money, and you said at that time you couldn't afford to do so."

"Oh, did I?" he said. And then he went on to tell me, making it appear just as if he had nothing to do with it and as if I were dealing with another firm, that I should go tell the treasurer who was in charge of the business office at that time that I was henceforth to get so much instead of what I had been getting. He made it appear that it was something that I had neglected.

This business association I entered into with a good deal of uncertainty and some little dread. I did not know Frohman, and I had been long with Daly. I was accustomed to his management and his way of producing plays.

I never had cause to regret my change in management. Charles Frohman was one of the fairest and squarest men I ever met.

On July 30, 1892, I appeared for the last time under the management of Augustin Daly at Stockwell's Theatre in San Francisco. The play was a revival of *A Night Off*, and I played my customary rôle of *Jack Mulberry*.

On October 3 of the same year I appeared as a star under the management of Charles Frohman at Palmer's Theatre, Broadway and Thirtieth Street. This had been Lester Wallack's Theatre, and after Palmer's management was renamed Wallack's.

CHAPTER TWENTY-ONE

MY early impression of Maude Adams, before it was finally decided that she was to be my leading woman in my first play as a star under the management of Charles Frohman, was that she looked too frail. I had been accustomed to play with Ada Rehan, who was so much bigger and stronger. Stronger she was, as was evidenced by the blow on the jaw that as *Katherine* she gave me in *The Taming of the Shrew*. In the scene, in the acting version, where *Petruchio* says:

Were it the forefoot of an angry bear,
I'd shake it off; but, as it's Kate's, I kiss it,

Katherine gives him a sound, ringing blow. There was a time when it was not considered good art actually to hit a person on the stage instead of making as if to hit; but there was no make-believe about this stage blow. It was indeed real; in fact, it seems to me now as I look back that the blow that *Katherine* used to give *Petruchio* might have given the redoubtable Dempsey a jolt.

169

Small wonder then that Maude Adams in her girlish slightness seemed to me too fragile for a leading woman. As a matter of fact she was never ill and never away from rehearsals in the years she played with me.

It was Mrs. Drew, my wife, who first suggested that Maude Adams become my leading woman. Maude Adams had been on the stage almost from childhood. Her mother was leading woman in the stock company at the Salt Lake Theatre. The family name was Kiskadden. Maude, herself, had appeared when quite young in Hoyt's play, *A Midnight Bell*. After that she left the stage to go to school.

As *Nell*, the consumptive factory girl, in an American adaptation of Ludwig Fulda's play, *The Lost Paradise*, she had made a hit. I saw her first, however, as *Evangeline Bender* in a farce which William Gillette had adapted from the French, called *All the Comforts of Home*. In this Forbes Robertson's brother, Ian, played an old, deaf fellow. The two things that I remember about the play are: the delicate charm of Maude Adams and the fact that all the other characters yelled at Ian Robertson.

When I was in San Francisco Maude Adams, who was playing at another theatre, came to the Baldwin

ELSIE DE WOLFE AS THE WAITING MAID, JOHN DREW AS THE COUNT, IN "A MARRIAGE OF CONVENIENCE"

ARTHUR BYRON AND JOHN DREW IN "THE TYRANNY OF TEARS"

Hotel to meet me. This appointment was the first time that I had seen her off the stage. I saw at once her alertness and her intelligence, and that she had a most expressive face.

The play selected for my first appearance under the new management was *The Masked Ball* by Alexandre Bisson and Albert Carré. This play took its name from the celebrated carnival, Veglione, which is held at Nice during the winter. The adaptation was made by young Clyde Fitch, whose play, *Beau Brummel*, had made so great an impression when played by Richard Mansfield. The cast was:

PAUL BLONDET	John Drew
JOSEPH POULARD	Harry Harwood
LOUIS MARTINOT	Harold Russell
M. BERGOMAT	C. Leslie Allen
CASIMIR	Frank E. Lamb
SUZANNE BLONDET	Maude Adams
MME. POULARD	Virginia Buchanan
MME. BERGOMAT	Annie Adams
ROSE	Lillian Florence

When I left Daly I assured him that, if ever the opportunity arose, I should be happy to make public acknowledgement of all that I felt that I owed him. It seemed to me that it was the only decent thing to do—to pay some tribute to the man who had taken so

The actor who played this part insisted upon saying, "No, no! Rubens bore me."

I said, thinking it was a slip of the tongue: "Why do you say that?"

He said: "Why not?"

Then I gathered he thought I meant by Rubens—country jays.

Finally, *Martinot* does see *Suzanne*.

"Did he say that I got tipsy?" she asks.

"Yes, he told me so; that's the reason I broke off the engagement."

Accordingly, at the end of the second act, she feigns tipsiness in order to shock the husband with whom she is really in love. It was admirably done, deliciously done. There was nothing vulgar about the scene; for, in the first place, she was not supposed to be intoxicated. Maude Adams did the whole episode daintily and with much charm. She carried a red rose which she would alternately smell and wave about. This was her own idea, and it was carried out very prettily.

The part of *Suzanne* established Maude Adams. She scored a greater success in my company as *Dorothy* in *Rosemary*, but after her performance in *The Masked Ball* there was no doubt of her ability and charm.

Before the Empire Theatre was built, the Frohman offices were at 1127 Broadway. I went there one day

MAUDE ADAMS AND JOHN DREW IN "ROSEMARY"

to see Frohman and was told by the office boy: "Mr. Frohman is out, and I don't know when he will be back."

"But I have an engagement with him," I protested.

"You will have to wait," said the boy.

I waited in the outer office, while Frohman waited for me inside.

Later, this same boy, whose name was Peter Daly, came to me at the suggestion of Charles Frohman as a dresser. He spent the day typewriting in the outer room of the Frohman offices and at night came to the theatre to dress me until I got a regular valet.

I was much surprised, some time after he left me, to learn that he was in a play and that his name was Arnold Daly. Of course he could not keep his own name, because Peter Dailey, later one of the popular players at Weber and Fields' Theatre, was then a well-known comedian playing in *The Country Sport* with May Irwin.

During the run of *The Masked Ball* I lived at the Marlborough Hotel, and in the side street Saint-Gaudens had a studio. I often went over and watched him work on the Sherman statue, which is now in the plaza at Fifty-ninth Street, New York. The model for the horse was the race horse Ontario.

When we played *The Masked Ball* in Washington,

Mrs. Ossian	Annie Adams
Suzanne-Elise	Olive May
Mrs. Beverly	
Stuart-Dodge	Kate Meek
Miriam	Maude Adams

The year after the World's Fair we were going to California with *Butterflies*. When we got near Chicago there was a great glare in the sky and we were told that the World's Fair buildings were burning.

At Hammond, which is some miles out of Chicago, we were compelled to get out of our Pullman, as there was a strike at the Pullman works. There was a sympathetic strike of the people working on the various roads, and Pullman cars were not allowed to go into Chicago.

We rode into Chicago by trolley. We were going straight to the Coast and not playing Chicago this trip. After we got off the trolley we had to take an elevated to get us to a place where we could get carriages to get across to the Northwestern station.

In getting on the elevated Maude Adams and the women of the company were nearly crushed to death. Great throngs of people were going to the fire and taking the trains right back again. The congestion was shocking. We were so much delayed that we missed

MAUDE ADAMS, ARTHUR BYRON, AND JOHN DREW IN "ROSEMARY"

our train and had to stay over a whole day until the same time next night.

The strikers were beginning to riot, and troops were brought down from Fort Sheridan and camped out on the Lake Front. I knew some of the officers and spent most of the day at this temporary camp. On our way West we were held up at different places by the striking people and those who sympathized with them, but they did not take our Pullman car off. We had to stop at night wherever we were, usually at some station we were passing through. It was very hot and we arrived at San Francisco two days late.

A familiar figure round the New York theatres in those days of the middle nineties was Charles Hoyt, the writer of many successful farces. The titles of these invariably began with the article "A"—*A Temperance Town*, *A Midnight Bell*, *A Contented Woman*, *A Stranger in New York*. Hoyt was a most amusing person. He came from New Hampshire, and he had an uncompromising Yankee accent. When he died he gave his place in New Hampshire to the Lambs Club in perpetuity, so that actors who had no place else to go might go there to stay.

One of the often-told stories about him was that on the first night that Goodwin was going to play Clyde

CHAPTER TWENTY-THREE

THE Empire Theatre which was so closely associated with the career of Charles Frohman and so important in my own career, as for so many years my season began there either on Labor Day or very close to that time, had been opened in January of 1893.

The opening play was *The Girl I Left Behind Me* by Franklin Fyles and David Belasco. This was just another version of Boucicault's play, *Jessie Brown*, or *The Relief of Lucknow*, with something of the good old classic, *Virginius*. The performance was given by the Empire Theatre stock company, and in the first cast were W. H. Thompson, William Morris, Orrin Johnson, Cyril Scott, Theodore Roberts, Sydney Armstrong, Odette Tyler and Katharine Florence.

After my own performance in *The Masked Ball* at the Standard Theatre at Thirty-third Street and Broadway, where we had moved when our time was up at Palmer's, I went up to the Empire to see the last few minutes of Charles Frohman's new production, *The Girl I Left Behind Me*, in the new theatre.

About two years after the opening I played at the Empire for the first time in Henry Arthur Jones' play, *The Bauble Shop*. The argument in this, and it seems quite unanswerable, was that the private immoralities of a statesman's life may be used by his enemies to defeat and humiliate him in public life. The play was more successful in New York than London.

I was *Viscount Clivebrooke*, the leader of the party in power, a cynical, brilliant statesman of forty-odd years, who indiscreetly falls in love with the daughter of a tippling toy-maker. J. E. Dodson played the toy-maker.

In all these early productions Frank E. Lamb was my stage manager. He had appeared with W. J. Florence in *The Mighty Dollar*. He was a son of Ed Lamb, who played for a long time in a stock company in Brooklyn, run by Mrs. F. B. Conway, who was the sister of Mrs. D. P. Bowers, my god-mother. In some of the early Daly plays Ed Lamb had played the low-comedy rôles on tour—the parts which James Lewis played in the original company.

Between *The Bauble Shop* and *Rosemary*, Maude Adams and I appeared in a number of plays. There was *That Imprudent Young Couple*, which had been tried out at the end of the season before. In this Henry Guy Carleton tried to repeat the gossamer success of

Butterflies, but failed. Then came *Christopher Jr.*, a bright but not altogether logical play by Madeline Lucette Ryley in which the players were:

CHRISTOPHER COLT, JR.	John Drew
CHRISTOPHER COLT, SR.	Harry Harwood
BERT BELLABY	Lewis Baker
HEDWAY	C. Leslie Allen
SIMPSON	Arthur Byron
GLIBB	Herbert Ayling
JOB	Joseph Humphreys
WHIMPER	Frank Lamb
MRS. GLIBB	Elsie De Wolfe
MRS. COLT	Anna Belmont
DORA	Maude Adams

We did an English version of *L'Ami des Femmes* by Dumas Fils. The adaptation was called *The Squire of Dames* and was made by R. C. Carton, the author of *Lord and Lady Algy*, *Lady Huntworth's Experiment* and many other successful plays.

AUDE ADAMS AND JOHN DREW IN MADELINE LUCETTE RYLEY'S COMEDY "CHRISTOPHER, JR."

CHAPTER TWENTY-FOUR

THE summer I was rehearsing *Rosemary* we were all living at Westhampton, Long Island—the James Lewises, my wife, mother and daughter, the three Barrymore children, and Henry Miller and his family.

One day, after a rehearsal of *Rosemary*, I was in a court of the Racquet Club when I was told that I was wanted on the telephone. I asked that the message be taken, but the servant came back to tell me that the person calling would not give the message. I put on a bathrobe and went to the telephone.

It was Henry Miller who was calling from Westhampton. He told me that James Lewis had had some trouble with his heart.

I asked: "Why don't you get a doctor?"

He answered, trying to break it to me gently: "There is no need for a doctor."

I didn't quite understand him. "What do you mean?"

He said: "There's nothing the matter with his heart now."

James Lewis had been my friend for twenty-odd years, ever since those old days at the Fifth Avenue Theatre when I first came to New York to play under Daly's management.

Much saddened I went on with the rehearsals of *Rosemary*. This play by Louis N. Parker and Murray Carson was one of the greatest successes I had. Only a few years ago I revived the play, and it was successful then.

In the first production Maude Adams made a tremendous hit as *Dorothy*. This rôle, which was the last she played with me, was the culminating thing in her early career, and it led to her being starred. The next season Frohman produced *The Little Minister*, with Maude Adams as *Lady Babbie*.

Charles Frohman probably thought that it was a great waste to leave in my company as leading woman an actress who had made so great a hit on her own account. Such delicate, almost spiritual, charm could be turned to great advantage in the proper plays.

The play *Rosemary* is not an extraordinary piece, but it does contain a great deal of proper sentiment, feeling and sympathy. It is gay and pretty, but not without depth.

Sir Jasper Thorndyke lives in his country place with only an old friend for a companion. A chaise contain-

EMPIRE THEATRE

CHARLES FROHMAN, RICH & HARRIS, Lessees.

CHARLES FROHMAN, Manager.

Also Manager of the Garrick and Garden Theatres.

WEEK COMMENCING MONDAY, SEPTEMBER 14, 1896.

Evenings at 8.20.   Matinee Saturday only.

Wednesday Matinees for the Season will be resumed September 23.

FIFTH SEASON OF THIS THEATRE.

AND FIFTH SEASON OF

Mr. JOHN DREW,

Under the management of CHARLES FROHMAN,

Presenting, for the first time in this country, a play, in four acts, entitled

ROSEMARY.

" That 's for remembrance."

By LOUIS N. PARKER and MURRAY CARSON.

SIR JASPER THORNDYKE	JOHN DREW
PROFESSOR JOGRAM	DANIEL HARKINS
CAPTAIN CRUICKSHANK, R. N	HARRY HARWOOD
WILLIAM WESTWOOD	ARTHUR BYRON
GEORGE MINIFIE	JOSEPH HUMPHREYS
ABRAHAM	FRANK LAMB
MRS. CRUICKSHANK	Mrs. ANNIE ADAMS
MRS. MINIFIE	Mrs. KING
PRISCILLA	ETHEL BARRYMORE
DOROTHY CRUICKSHANK	MAUDE ADAMS

ACT I.—HIGH-ROAD. EXTERIOR OF SIR JASPER THORNDYKE'S PARK.
Sir Jasper makes a mistake.

ACT II.—DINING-ROOM AT INGLE HALL.
Sir Jasper makes amends.

ACT III.—UPPER ROOM IN MRS. MINIFIE'S COFFEE-HOUSE, IN LONDON.
Sir Jasper forgets.

ACT IV.—SAME ROOM AS ACT III., BUT FIFTY YEARS HAVE ELAPSED.
Sir Jasper remembers.

Costumes by DAZIAN.   Gowns by HELEN WINDSOR.

Scenery by E. G. UNITT.

Incidental Music by W. W. FURST.

Stage direction of JOSEPH HUMPHREYS.

EMPIRE THEATRE ORCHESTRA.
WM FURST, Musical Director.

Overture—" Fingal's Cave "	Mendelssohn
Paraphrase—" How Fair Art Thou "	Nevvadba
" Album Leaf "	Wagner
Menuet—" L'Arlesienne "	Bizet
Waltz—" Les Patineurs "	E. Waldteufel
Gavotte—" L'Ingenue "	Arditi

From Theatre Collection, Harvard University.

**DOROTHY WAS THE LAST PART MAUDE ADAMS PLAYED AS LEADING
WOMAN WITH JOHN DREW**

ing a runaway couple breaks down directly outside of the place of *Sir Jasper*, and he takes the youthful lovers into his house. He falls in love with the girl, *Dorothy*. *Professor Jogram*, his friend, tries to show him the folly of his falling in love with someone so much younger than himself. *Jasper* sees her happily married to the young lover, *Ensign Westford*, and he returns to his bachelor ways. He outlives them both and at the Diamond Jubilee he finds in the very house where he had taken *Dorothy* to see the Coronation, a souvenir of his romance. In this last act, which is really a monologue, *Sir Jasper*, who is on the verge of senility, reminisces at length.

My niece, Ethel Barrymore, was cast for the rustic maid, *Priscilla*, in *Rosemary*. She had a dress and shoes which might have made another young girl seem grotesque. However, in spite of this most unbecoming attire, her beauty made a great impression. *Priscilla*, the maid, was really her first appearance in New York, though she had substituted in my company in *The Bauble Shop*. One night when Elsie De Wolfe was ill, Ethel Barrymore appeared as *Kate Fennell*, though she was not announced on the program.

When *Rosemary* had run a hundred nights, a silver cup was given as a souvenir; this custom has long since been done away with. The cup bore the name of the

MRS. JOHN DREW, SENIOR, AS MRS. MALAPROP IN "THE RIVALS"

play, the occasion and the quotation: "That's for re-membrance." I never thought of these cups again until a few years ago, when I was playing the revival of *Rosemary* in San Francisco. The property man of the Columbia Theatre told me that there was a woman who had one of these cups which she found under some debris near the site of the Baldwin Hotel just after the fire. I told the property man that I would like to have the cup, if the owner would part with it. He secured it for me. It looks more like pewter than silver today, and there is a hole punched through the bottom of it.

In the late nineties I saw my mother act for the last time, in Chicago. This was in an all-star cast of *The Rivals*. She played her familiar character of *Mrs. Malaprop*. William H. Crane was *Sir Anthony;* Robert Taber, *Captain Absolute;* Joseph Jefferson, *Bob Acres;* Nat Goodwin, *Sir Lucius;* Joseph Holland, *Faukland;* Edward Holland, *Fag;* Francis Wilson, *David;* Julia Marlowe, *Lydia Languish;* and Fanny Rice, *Lucy*. This cast made a celebrated and quick tour through the important Eastern cities, playing in about twenty-seven different towns in less than a month.

I was playing *Rosemary* in another theatre in Chi-cago and on Sunday night between the Chicago and

Milwaukee engagements of *The Rivals* I gave a dinner for the cast at The Annex. Ethel Barrymore, who was in my company at the time, was present at the dinner. Jefferson and my mother, who had seen so much of the early days of the American theatre, told a great many stories of the old days.

The following year I was playing in Salt Lake City in the road tour of *Rosemary*, when I received word that my mother had died at Larchmont.

At the time, Ethel Barrymore was playing with Henry Irving in London. They were rehearsing a new play. She returned to the afternoon rehearsal late, and she told Irving that she had been to send a cable; her grandmother was dead.

Irving excused her from rehearsal. "Mrs. John Drew," he said, "was the finest actress in her line that I have ever seen."

After the road tour of *Rosemary*, Isabel Irving played *Dorothy* part of the time. I appeared at the Empire Theatre in *A Marriage of Convenience*, adapted by Sydney Grundy from *Un Mariage sous Louis XV*. I played the part of the count who falls in love with his young wife less than three days after the wedding. Isabel Irving made her first appearance as my leading lady in New York as the young countess. Of course, I had played with her often before at Daly's, and she had played the leading part opposite me in *The Cabinet Minister*, when Ada Rehan refused to play it. Elsie DeWolfe played the waiting maid in *A Marriage of Convenience*.

When the Spanish-American War broke out, I very much wanted to go, and I applied in person to Theodore Roosevelt, who was then organizing a regiment of cavalry. I had known him when he was police commissioner in New York. I met him at lunch one day at Delmonico's with Richard Harding Davis; when I joined them they were having a heated but friendly argument about something or other. I don't remember what it was about, but they were both much excited.

The day I saw Roosevelt at the war department in Washington he told me that both Henry Cabot Lodge and I were too old to think of going to war, that we knew nothing of warfare and that I had a wife and child to support. I had not the moral courage to point out to him that he had four or five children.

Then came *One Summer's Day* by Henry V. Esmond, which was not a great success and was followed by one of my biggest successes, Henry Arthur Jones' play, *The Liars*. In this sparkling comedy I played *Sir Christopher Deering*, the friend of everybody and the preserver of family honor.

In the last act *Sir Christopher*, who has been devoting his time and ingenuity for four days and four acts to the seemingly futile attempt to prevent the elopement of his closest friend with the silly young wife of a common acquaintance, confronts them in his apartment. The hour is late, and *Sir Christopher* is getting ready to start for Africa to rejoin his regiment, the next day. Moreover, he has just asked a charming young woman to be his wife. He has little time to spare, but in a long speech which is very effective he sets facts before these two, the heedless man and the vain woman, and convinces them of their folly.

On the first night of *The Liars* the curtain failed to come down after the first act. The stage manager said that he had given both the warning bell, which means to get ready, and the second bell, which is the signal to ring down. The flyman in charge of the curtain said he heard only the one signal, so did not ring down. This spoiled the first act.

In the second act a hand organ is supposed to be played outside, so that the heroine can get rid of the young man by sending him out to give some money to the monkey. When the cue came there was no music from the hand organ. The property man, wishing to prevent the possibility of any tampering with the hand organ, had removed the handle, and then in his first-

JOHN DREW AND FRANK LAMB IN HENRY ARTHUR JONES' COMEDY,
"THE LIARS"

night excitement he forgot to come back to turn the handle.

Isabel Irving, who was playing *Lady Jessica*, was at a loss for a few seconds but quickly sent Arthur Byron, the young man, for a glass of water. Notwithstanding these two accidents, the play was a great success that first night and for months to come.

The cast was:

CHRISTOPHER DEERING	John Drew
EDWARD FALKNER	Arthur Byron
GILBERT NEPEAN	D. H. Harkins
GEORGE NEPEAN	Orrin Johnson
FREDDIE TATTON	Lewis Baker
ARCHIBALD COKE	Harry Harwood
MRS. CRESPIN	Marie Derickson
BEATRICE EBERNOE	Blanche Burton
DOLLY COOKE	Elizabeth Tyree
FERRIS	Clara Hunter
LADY ROSAMOND TATTON	Annie Irish
LADY JESSICA NEPEAN	Isabel Irving

CHAPTER TWENTY-FIVE

AFTER I left the Daly company I saw my old manager now and again. In the middle nineties his former program of light comedies and revivals of the old comedies had become less popular, and he was forced to make concessions to the popular taste. One of his last successes was an English melodrama, *The Great Ruby*.

The last time that I saw Augustin Daly was at the Continental Hotel in Paris. Ada Rehan was stopping with the Dalys. My card was sent up and, in the very casual manner of French hotels, was left at the Daly apartment. Daly came down; he was very cordial and nice. I had just come from Lake Como, and I told Daly that I had been to Cadenabbia, which is supposed to be the place which *Claude Melnotte* in *The Lady of Lyons* describes to *Pauline* in the speech that begins:

"Nay, dearest, nay, if thou wouldst have me paint the home."

"I suppose you felt like playing the character?" asked Daly.

"I'm afraid, Governor, that that's about the only

place where I'd ever be allowed to play *Claude Melnotte*."

A year or so later I was in Dresden, waiting for my daughter's school to close before the summer vacation, and we got the news that Augustin Daly had died in Paris.

When the Daly company disbanded Mrs. Gilbert came under the management of Charles Frohman and appeared with Annie Russell in Jerome K. Jerome's *Miss Hobbs* and Captain Marshall's play, *The Royal Family*. Then Charles Frohman decided to star her, and Clyde Fitch was commissioned to write a play for her called *Granny*.

This was produced with Marie Doro in the supporting cast at the Lyceum Theatre. At the end of the play Mrs. Gilbert recited an epilogue which referred to the old Daly days and to Ada Rehan, James Lewis and myself. This might have been pleasant and proper on the first night, but it seemed rather strange to continue it through the run of the piece.

As the midweek matinee at the Lyceum did not conflict with my own, I was able to see *Granny*, and after the performance I saw Mrs. Gilbert in her dressing room. Nearly thirty years before we had played together for the first time at the Fifth Avenue Theatre.

At a supper party Augustin Daly gave one year for

Henry Irving and Ellen Terry at Delmonico's I kissed Mrs. Gilbert's hand as I entered. She was not in the bill we were then playing at the theatre, and I had not seen her for some time.

Irving, probably thinking that it was rather a formal greeting for people who saw each other every day, said: "You don't always do that, do you?"

"No, I usually do this." And I kissed her on the cheek.

This delightful old lady had been "grandma" to us all and had been on the stage many years. During the run of *Granny* she died.

After Augustin Daly died, Ada Rehan played in Paul Kester's play, *Sweet Nell of Old Drury*, and with Otis Skinner in revivals of some of the old Daly successes. I did not see her in any of these productions.

The last time I saw her was at her house in Ninety-third Street. She was ill then and had aged a great deal in appearance; but I do not believe either of us thought that it was our last meeting. Our conversation was more reminiscent than it had been before. We talked of those youthful days at the Arch Street Theatre and the very early Daly days.

Ada Rehan had a fine mind; she was a great actress and she had a sweet soul.

CHAPTER TWENTY-SIX

THE season of 1899 and 1900 I played that delightful comedy, *The Tyranny of Tears*, by C. Haddon Chambers. This was one of the finest light comedies that I played. I revived it a few years ago, and it was equally successful then. When it was revived Chambers came over and made certain changes in the play to shorten it somewhat. There were certain scenes that were really unnecessary. In the last act some of the dialogue between the girl secretary and *Parbury's* friend were cut out. This did not disturb the play or the continuity of the action. It was done so that I might play the same evening Barrie's play, *The Will*. This bill was one of the most attractive that I ever played.

The rôle of *Parbury*, the novelist, in *The Tyranny of Tears* was a most grateful one. Isabel Irving was very good as the wife, and Ida Conquest made a great hit as *Hyacinth Woodward*, the novelist's amanuensis. In the revival Laura Hope Crewes was the wife and Mary Boland the secretary.

The original cast was:

PARBURY	John Drew
GEORGE GUNNING	Arthur Byron
ARMITAGE	Harry Harwood
EVANS	Frank Lamb
HYACINTH	Ida Conquest
MRS. PARBURY	Isabel Irving

The next year I left light comedy for dramatized fiction. As Frohman did not have a play for me, I played *Richard Carvel*, a dramatization of Winston Churchill's book by E. E. Rose.

"C. F." asked me to come up to his farm, Hidden Brook Farm at Mount Kisco. He read me the dramatization. "What do you think of that?" he asked.

I didn't know; nor did I know at that time that the play had been written with James K. Hackett in mind. Charles Frohman had bribed or cajoled his brother Dan into giving this thing up to him for me. Hackett would have been ideal for the character. I was never happy in it. It was out of my sphere, and I was too old for the young hero.

The surprising thing of my tour in this piece is that it made a good deal of money. I suppose this was due to the popularity of the book, for the play was not a very good one.

The cast for this dramatization was:

RICHARD CARVEL	John Drew
LIONEL CARVEL	Herbert Carr
LORD COMYN	Arthur Byron
DUKE OF CHARTERSEA	Frank Losee
MARMADUKE MANNERS	Harry Harwood
GRAFTON CARVEL	Lewis Baker
CAPTAIN LEWIS	Dodson Mitchell
HORACE WALPOLE	Francis Powers
CHARLES FOX	Brandon Tynan
DOROTHY MANNERS	Ida Conquest
PATTY SWAIN	Olive May
MRS. MANNERS	Mrs. W. G. Jones

At supper one night in Chicago Sarah Bernhardt asked me whether I would like to come to Paris and act in a play that she was thinking of doing. Sarah Bernhardt's companion, a little woman, who not only was her companion, but played parts in the company, and a man from the French paper, *Figaro*, were also present, and the conversation was carried on in French.

I was very diffident about my French—that is, the thought of going to Paris to play in French made me feel diffident. "But my French is not good enough," I said in answer to her query.

She said: "You speak French very well."

"Yes, that's all right—the fluency of it perhaps, but not the accent."

"Oh, that won't matter. This is an Englishman you are going to play."

Apparently Madame Bernhardt had not a very high regard for the English fashion of speaking French.

My niece, Ethel Barrymore, played a few parts in my company, played with Irving in his familiar repertoire in London and played Jessie Milward's part in a road company of Captain Marshall's play *His Excellency, the Governor*. Then Charles Frohman decided to star her in Clyde Fitch's play, *Captain Jinks*. This play of New York life just after the Civil War, with costumes inspired by Godey's Ladies Book and scenes in the Brevoort House, made a great impression when it was produced in New York.

Before it came to the Garrick Theatre, it was tried out at the Walnut Street Theatre in Philadelphia, the oldest theatre in the country. Twenty years ago at the Walnut there was an old-fashioned, regular gallery audience, keen to approve of what it liked and quick to voice its disapproval. My niece, playing for the first time a long and important rôle, was somewhat nervous and not quite audible.

A friendly voice called to her from the gallery: "Speak up, Ethel. You're all right. The Drews is all good actors."

ETHEL BARRYMORE AS THE RUSTIC MAID IN "ROSEMARY"

CHAPTER TWENTY-SEVEN

WHEN we were playing *The Duke of Killi-crankie* at the National Theatre in Washington, President Roosevelt sent for me to come into his box during one of the intermissions. He and his party were in the box usually reserved for the President, and it has a small withdrawing room back of it. I had supposed that he would see me in this room. Instead, when he greeted me he drew me through the secret service men who were sitting at the back. With him were Mrs. Roosevelt, two of the Roosevelt children and Mrs. Henry Cabot Lodge.

I felt much perturbed to be before an audience on the wrong side of the curtain. It did not occur to President Roosevelt at all that I should have any diffidence about coming before people with my make-up on. His greeting was most hearty, and he liked the play.

The last time I heard from him was a few weeks before he died, when he wrote me: "Just to wish you many happy New Years, John Drew; from an old friend and admirer."

Theodore Roosevelt's successor, President Taft, also brought me to the front of a box in my make-up. We were playing *The Perplexed Husband* by Alfred Sutro at the Empire Theatre in New York, when President Taft asked me to come into the box. His party had arrived late and was not seen by the audience when they were ushered into the theatre. The lights were turned on, and I appeared in the box just as the audience recognized the President.

Captain Marshall wrote two very delightful comedies in which I played, *The Second in Command* and *The Duke of Killicrankie*.

The Second in Command served me for two seasons. This play was the first time that khaki was used on the stage; that is, it was the first exposition of khaki on the stage in a military sense. Guy Standing, who was knighted for his services in the British Navy during the recent war, was extremely good as *Colonel Anstruther*.

My nephew, Lionel Barrymore, who played the part of a young officer in this play made a pleasing impression, but the following season, as the Neapolitan organ grinder in *The Mummy and the Humming Bird* his work was a revelation.

The original cast of *The Second in Command* was:

LIEUT. COL. MILES ANSTRUTHER, D. S. O.	Guy Standing
MAJOR CHRISTOPHER BINGHAM	John Drew
LIEUTENANT SIR WALTER MANNERING	Oswald Yorke
LIEUTENANT BARKER	Lionel Barrymore
MEDENHEM	Reginald Carrington
HARTOPP	Robert Schable
SERGEANT	George Harcourt
CORPORAL	Percy Smith
ORDERLY	George Ford
MR. FENWICK	Lewis Baker
THE HON. HILDEBRAND CARSTAIRS	Hassard Short
THE DUKE OF HULL	Robert Mackay
MURIEL MANNERING	Ida Conquest
LADY HARBURGH	Ida Vernon
NORAH VINING	Caroline Keeler

The Duke of Killicrankie was a very fine, light comedy in which four sharply contrasted characters are thrown together. These were played by that famous English actress, Fannie Brough, Margaret Dale, Ferdinand Gottschalk and myself.

The complete cast was:

THE DUKE	John Drew
HENRY PITT WELBY	Ferdinand Gottschalk
AMBROSE HICKS	Lewis Baker
BUTLER	Robert Schable
ALEXANDER MACBAYNE	Reginald Carrington

FOOTMAN	B. W. Parmenter
COUNTESS OF PANGBOURNE	Kate Lester
LADY HENRIETTA ADDISON	Margaret Dale
MRS. MULHOLLAND	Fannie Brough
MRS. MACBAYNE	Constance Bell

The summer before I appeared in *Captain Dieppe* by Anthony Hope and Edward Rose, I met the two authors in London. We had lunch together, and Anthony Hope said to Rose: "You tell the story of *Captain Dieppe*."

Rose replied: "No, I told it the last time."

Finally after some little arguing between them, they told me the story of this play, and it sounded fairly reasonable. When it was presented, it did not have the quality of an Anthony Hope story, and it was not a success.

Elizabeth Marbury, who was Anthony Hope's agent, sent him a cable after the first performance in Providence where the play was tried out. "Play apparently pleased Providence public." I asked Miss Marbury afterwards whether she thought the alliteration would have any convincing power with Anthony Hope.

In that same early season in a play of Clyde Fitch's called *Glad of It*, in which my nephew, John Barrymore, had a small part, there was a conversation between two shop girls.

"Where are you going tonight, dearie?"

"Why, to see John Drew in *Captain Dippy*."

Unfortunately for this play, they did not have to change the line for *Glad of It* was an even greater failure than *Captain Dieppe*.

The season of Augustus Thomas's play, *De Lancey*, in which Doris Keane, Walter Hale, Margaret Dale and Guy Nichols played with me, we were booked to open New Year's day at the Hollis Street Theatre in Boston. There was no morning train at that time which we could count on getting us to Boston in time for the matinee.

Every year on the anniversary of the opening of The Players—New Year's Eve—there is celebrated Founders' Night. I very much wished to attend this year, especially as it was the first year that I was president of the club.

Through the influence of a friend in the railroad business I was given permission to have a private car containing my company—several of the men were members of The Players and also wanted to be there that night—attached to the newspaper and mail train that arrives in Boston early in the morning.

We had the most uncomfortable train ride and arrived early, far out in the yards. We went to our hotels, where we learned that we were not booked to play a holiday matinee. New Year's Day was not at that time a holiday in the state of Massachusetts. The company manager had not taken the trouble to consult the Frohman office. He took it for granted that we were to play a matinee.

CHAPTER TWENTY-EIGHT

MY season at the Empire Theatre under the management of Charles Frohman usually opened on Labor Day or very close to that day. I played a varying number of weeks in New York and then went on tour. Our itinerary on the road was much the same, except that we did not go to the Coast every year. One year we would go to New Orleans, playing Richmond, Charleston, Savannah and the intervening towns on our way, and the next year we would go to the Coast.

The year that we did *My Wife*, a comedy by Michael Morton from the French of *Devault et Charnay*, we went both South and West. We reached the Coast just at the time the fleet came into San Francisco; that was the year that Roosevelt sent the fleet around the world. There was a great deal of enthusiasm and a good deal of entertaining for the officers and men. I knew a great many of the commanders, and we visited several of the ships for lunch.

We were playing in the Van Ness Theatre, a theatre which was built hurriedly after the fire. It seated an enormous number of people. It had a corrugated-iron roof and when the summer trade winds came up during the matinee they rattled the roof so much that the audience could barely hear what was said on the stage.

My Wife did an enormous business in San Francisco that year, as it had done everywhere on the road. In all the towns that we visited, Billie Burke, who was my leading woman, was acclaimed as a charming actress and a beautiful woman. She played *Beatrice Dupré*. The cast for *My Wife* was:

GERALD EVERSLIGH	John Drew
THE HON. GIBSON GORE.	Ferdinand Gottschalk
CAPTAIN PUTNAM FREZBY	Walter Soderling
M. DUPRÉ	Morton Selten
BARON GORANCLOS	Albert Roccardi
M. VALBORNE	Mario Majeroni
M. POTIN	Axel Bruun
DAVIES	Herbert Budd
CROCKER	Rex McDougal
HEADWAITER	E. Soldene Powell
RENE FLANDERS	Frank Goldsmith
PORTER	L. C. Howard
BEATRICE DUPRÉ	Billie Burke
MIRIAM HAWTHORNE	Dorothy Tenant
MRS. DENHAM FANE	Ida Greeley Smith
BARONES GRANCLOS	Hope Latham
MADAM DUPRÉ	Mrs. Kate Pattison Selten
MARIE	May Gayler

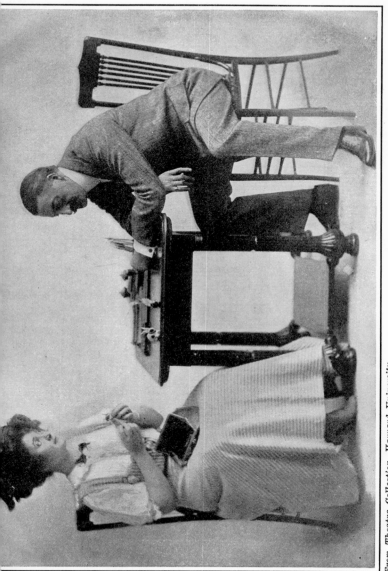

From *Theatre Collection, Harvard University.*

JOHN DREW AND BILLIE BURKE IN "MY WIFE"

This play introduced Billie Burke to American audiences.

In this play I was the guardian of *Beatrice*, who runs away from a school and suddenly appears at my place. We go to Switzerland, and I gradually fall in love with her. On our return we are married.

Someone sent out some press stuff that I was not only her guardian in the play, but that I had some years before made a pact with her father, whose name also was Billie Burke, that, in case of his death, I would look out for his daughter. Of course there was no truth in this statement, and Billie Burke became my leading woman because she had done well in some Frohman plays in London. Charles Frohman was much pleased with her reception in this country, and the following year he starred her in *Love Watches*.

One night just after the play in San Francisco, word was brought into my dressing room that Mr. Daly wanted to see me. I did not know anyone named Daly in the city at that time, nor could I place him when a large, powerful-looking Chinaman wearing American clothes was ushered into my room.

"You don't remember Lu Lung, Mr. Drew," he said without any accent.

Then I remembered that on one of our trips to the Coast years before, Augustin Daly had bought a little Chinaman from his parents for a period of three years. For a while Lu Lung Daly, dressed in beautiful Chinese clothes, had given out the programs in the lobby of Daly's Theatre, and Augustin Daly was greatly pleased with his contract; but he became very tired of the little Chinaman and got too much of him in his household and in his employ.

Daly never found a way to get out of the arrangement which he had made with the boy's parents, and it used to amuse the rest of us a great deal; for he never found any difficulty in getting rid of anyone else connected with the theatre. He was forced to support the boy for the entire period.

Now he stood before me, recalling the old days and telling me of Chinatown where, from his own talk, he seemed to be something of a power.

"But why do you call yourself Daly?" I asked.

"I was Daly—Lu Lung Daly—when I knew you, and I thought you would remember me that way."

Earlier that same season I had been playing in Louisville the first three days of the week, and E. H. Sothern was to follow me for the last three. Before I left town Sothern arrived, and we met in the corridor of the hotel. We were joined by a very dignified old gentleman, who was evidently a citizen of the town.

He came up, bowed and said to Sothern: "Mr. Mansfield, I am very glad to see you here, and I'm going to be delighted to attend every performance of yours during your all too brief sojourn. I have watched your career, Mr. Mansfield."

The citizen of Louisville shook hands with Sothern again and walked away.

"Why, in heaven's name, didn't you say something?" I asked.

"What was there to say?" said Sothern.

"He doesn't know that Dick Mansfield is dead," I went on.

"Well," said Sothern, "that doesn't hurt me so much. He doesn't know that I'm alive."

CHAPTER TWENTY-NINE

I PLAYED two plays by W. Sommerset Maugham:
Smith and *Jack Straw*. *Smith*, in which Mary
Boland played the title part, was a success from the
beginning.

The cast of *Smith* was:

THOMAS FREEMAN	John Drew
HERBERT DALLAS-BAKER K. C.	Morton Selten
ALGERNON PEPPERCORN	Hassard Short
FLETCHER	Louis Casson
MRS. DALLAS BAKER	Isabel Irving
EMILY CHAPMAN	Sibil Thorndike
MRS. OTTO ROSENBERG	Jane Laurel
SMITH	Mary Boland

Jack Straw, which like *Smith* had a great success,
had this cast:

JACK STRAW	John Drew
AMBROSE HOLLAND	Edgar L. Davenport
LORD SERLO	Frank Goldsmith
COUNT ADRIAN VON BREMER	Mario Majeroni
MR. PARKE JENNINGS	Fred Tyler
VINCENT, his son	Edwin Nicander
REV. LEWIS ABBOTT	E. Soldene Powell

From Theatre Collection, Harvard University.

FROM LEFT TO RIGHT: HASSARD SHORT, JANE LAUREL, MORTON SELTEN, MARY BOLAND, ISABEL IRVING, JOHN DREW, AND SIBYL THORNDIKE IN W. SOMMERSET MAUGHAM'S COMEDY, "SMITH"

MRS. PARKE JENNINGS	Rose Coghlan
ETHEL, her daughter	Mary Boland
LADY WANLEY	Adelaide Prince
ROSIE ABBOTT	Kate Kimball
MRS. WITHERS	Grace Henderson

In the company there were also a number of amateurs who walked on and took places at tables in the restaurant scene. One of the young men had nothing to do except to walk to a table with a young woman, to be told by the head waiter to go to another table, and then, after they had moved, only to be told that they must move again. They are supposed to be very irate at this. It was all dumb show.

When we were on tour we reached the native town of this young man, and the papers in advance had some small notices about him and that he was a member of my company.

"It's too bad," I told him, "that you are making your first appearance in your home town as a mere figure."

I wrote him some lines, so that this friendly audience could see him do something more than merely walk on and so that he could say that he had acted in a play.

The night of the performance came. The house was full of his friends, and they gave him a great reception, so great that he forgot all the lines that I had written for him.   He just went through the dumb show as usual.

Sudden loss of memory in the theatre is not uncommon, and it is often tragic in its consequences.   But there is an amusing story of an old actor who had been out of a job for a long time. Finally, he obtained a small part which, for anyone of experience, should have been easily learned.

In the play he had a speech in which he advises his son to be very diligent and persistent.   This fatherly advice ended with the good old adage that "time is money."

When he got to this line on the opening night he said: "Don't forget that time is——"   He paused, coughed and appealed to the prompter, who answered in an audible whisper: "Money."

The old actor: "Oh, yes—time is money."

The deduction was that it had been so long since he had had any money that he had forgotten that it existed.

My daughter, Louise Drew, and I were riding in Central Park one afternoon in December of the year that I was playing *Inconstant George* at the Empire. My mare stumbled and, while I was trying to get her

on her feet again, she fell.   Before I could disengage
my feet from the stirrups she rolled over me.   My
collar bone was broken, my shoulder fractured and
the ligaments in my right leg twisted.

My daughter was wearing a safety riding skirt, but
for some unknown reason it refused to work when she
tried to dismount, and she was caught on the pommel.
She finally disengaged herself, and a mounted police-
man, to whom she had called, came up.   I was taken
to the Presbyterian Hospital, where Dr. Joseph Blake
set my shoulder.

While I was in the hospital I received a letter from
Frederick Remington, the painter:

> See by paper you are on the mend.   You know
> I have a life sentence to walk on one leg because
> of a horse, so I can sympathize.   You don't have
> to walk on your hands, but you will have to be
> easy when you "muscle out" chairs as you once
> did so grandly.
>
> I have observed that a man don't have so much
> glue in the seat of his pants at 40 as at 20.   All
> those in favor of this motion say, "How!"

When I came out of the hospital Frederick Remington was dead.

I attended the horse show in Madison Square Garden with Frederick Remington one time.   We were

standing at the ring watching a man we both knew riding a horse over some hurdles. When this rider passed us I could hear Remington muttering imprecations under his breath.

"What's the matter with you?" I asked. "You know Frank very well. Don't you like him?"

"Of course I like him. He's a fine fellow. But I used to be able to do that once," Remington said plaintively. By that time he had become quite stout.

After some weeks I returned to playing, and I opened my season in Boston with *Inconstant George*, the play I had been doing before. This adaptation from the French of L'Ane de Buridan was never so successful in this country as it was afterwards in England, where Charles Hawtrey played the leading part, that of a man of many love affairs who falls victim to a young woman at last.

The American cast for *Inconstant George* was:

GEORGE BULLIN	John Drew
LUCIAN DeVERSANNES	Martin Sabine
MORLAND	Fred Tilden
ADOLPHEUS	Rex McDougal
GIRAND	W. Soderling
BUTLER	Bernard Fairfax
PAGE BOY	Robert Schable
MICHELINE	Mary Boland
ODETTE DE VERSANNES	Adelaide Prince

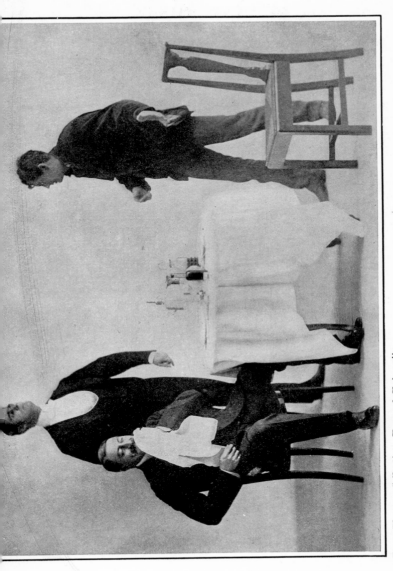

JOHN DREW, REGINALD CARRINGTON, AND LIONEL BARRYMORE IN "THE MUMMY AND THE HUMMING BIRD"

FANCHON CHANCELLE	Jane Laurel
VIVETTE LAMBERT	Desmond Kelly
BARONESS STECKE	Marie Berkeley
MADAM DE LAMOND	Carlotta Doty
LOUISE	Alice Soderling

After I left the Daly company I played but one Shakespearian character, *Benedick*, in *Much Ado About Nothing*. I had always wanted to play this character, and when Maude Adams and I were playing together I wanted her to play *Beatrice*. We talked about it a great deal, but it was years afterwards before I finally played *Benedick*, and Laura Hope Crewes was the *Beatrice*.

In this Shakespearian revival the cast was:

DON PEDRO	Frank Kemble Cooper
DON JOHN	Frank Elliott
CLAUDIO	Fred Eric
BENEDICK	John Drew
LEONATO	Henry Stephenson
ANTONIO	Sidney Herbert
BATHAZAR	Nigel Barry
CONRADE	Herbert Delmore
BORACHIO	Edward Longman
FRIAR FRANCIS	Bertram Marburgh
DOGBERRY	Hubert Druce
VERGES	Malcolm Bradley
A SEXTON	Walter Soderling
OATCAKE	Rexford Kendrick
SEACOLE	Murray Ross
HERO	Mary Boland

BEATRICE	Laura Hope Crewes
MARGARET	Florence Harrison
URSULA	Alice John

Frohman did not care much about the Shakespearian comedy, but he was not unwilling that I should play *Benedick*. I suppose that I had been away from this style of comedy too long—more than twenty years; in any event, the production was not a success, and the acting was not up to the standard set in the Daly productions of Shakespeare. This revival was withdrawn and my old success, *The Tyranny of Tears*, with Barrie's fine play in three scenes, *The Will*, used as an afterpiece.

Joseph H. Choate, while ambassador to England, had always been extremely kind and gracious to my niece, Ethel Barrymore, and myself when we were in London. I always had a lively recollection of this kindness, and one day when I was walking down Fifth Avenue I saw before me a somewhat bowed figure, which I recognized to be that of Choate.

I overtook him and said: "Do you remember me, Mr. Choate?"

He looked at me for a moment and said: "Good God, it's Drew."

"I said: "It is."

"Mercy, why don't you grow old?" he asked.

It was then some years since our meetings in London. I replied: "I don't know, Mr. Choate, unless I can explain in the words of old *Mr. Adam* in *As You Like It*, who says: 'Never in my youth did I apply hot and rebellious liquors in my blood.' "

He looked at me quizzically under his bushy eyebrows and asked: "Drew, is that entirely true?"

I laughed with him and said: "No, sir, it isn't. That's what quotations are for."

He patted me on the shoulder, and we parted.

In these years as a Frohman star I also played Pinero's fine play, *His House in Order*, in which Margaret Illington gave a splendid performance and for this the cast was:

HILARY JESSON	John Drew
FILMER JESSON, M. P.	C. M. Hallard
DEREK JESSON	Leona Powers
SIR DANIEL RIDGELEY	Arthur Elliot
PRYCE RIDGELEY	Martin Sabine
MAJOR MAUREWARDE	Henry Vibart
DR. DILNOTT	Herbert Budd
HARDING	Gilbert Douglas
FORSHAW	Rex McDougal
SERVANTS	Maurice Franklyn
	Henry Fearing
NINA	Margaret Illington
LADY RIDGELEY	Lena Halliday
GERALDINE RIDGELEY	Madge Girdlestone
MLLE. THOME	Hope Latham

look on his face. He put it down by the young woman with us who tasted it and exclaimed: "They've heated it."

It turned out afterwards that it had been milked out of a goat in the back yard. My courier was at that time downstairs having his drinks, so I asked the young proprietor in Italian for some ice to put in the milk, and he laughed. I thought he was laughing at my Italian, but he said: "Say, bo, you might as well ask me for a gold mine over here."

Of course consternation and astonishment were registered by all of us.

I said: "Where did you get that Second Avenue East Side English?"

"I lived there," he said.

"Aren't you Italian?"

"Yes, I was; but I went over there with me parents." He had lived all his life on the East Side.

I said: "What are you doing here?"

"Well," he said, "me uncle bought this place."

His uncle, it seems, had gone to the United States years before and had made some money in a restaurant. He had bought this inn when he had made enough money to do so. It was rather an historic place in a way.

"Are you going to stay here?"

JOHN DREW AT EASTHAMPTON, LONG ISLAND

KYALAMI, JOHN DREW'S HOUSE AT EASTHAMPTON

"Naw. Me mother's coming over soon, and when she does, me for the big city."

The whole thing struck me as very extraordinary. "When you get back to the big city you must come and see me," I said.

He asked: "What's your name?"

I told him.

"Sure," he said, "I know you. You got a cigar factory there."

He referred of course to a five-cent cigar that was named after me without my consent.

It was more flattering even than the occasion when Lewis and I were recognized by the impudent child in the garden at Hamburg.

When we got to Amalfi, just after we had had lunch, Burton Holmes turned up. He greeted us and said: "I've just met a friend of yours a few miles back. He says he knows you very well."

I said: "Was it the proprietor of the inn at Positano?"

Holmes said that he had been looking over the register, which was very old and interesting. In it he saw the names of our party.

"There's somebody I know," Holmes said to the proprietor of the inn.

"He was here today."

CHAPTER THIRTY-ONE

IN the revival of *Rosemary*, I was booked to appear for one night in the Metropolitan Theatre at Rochester, Minnesota, the home of the Mayo brothers. When I reached the theatre I found it was a horrible hole. The condition of things behind the scenes was shocking, to say the least. I was infuriated with my stage manager, because he hadn't told me about the theatre. He had gone there during the day in time to have had something done. At least there might have been some cleaning done.

I wrote to the health officer, who happened to be one of the Mayo brothers, and told him of the desperate condition of the theatre. He went with the mayor of the town to see the place and ordered the theatre closed until it should be renovated and cleaned.

I had a feeling that I had not done myself any good, for I had to give my performance, but that I had bettered the place for the next touring company. I wrote to Charles Frohman about the matter, and the last letter I ever received from him informed me that this

PAVLOWA AND JOHN DREW, AT THE TIME OF THE REVIVAL OF "ROSEMARY"

theatre was scratched by his office, Klaw and Erlanger and others.

I did not see Charles Frohman before he sailed on the "Lusitania," but when I was in Anaconda I received a letter from him telling me that he was sailing very shortly. Alf Hayman, who owned the Empire Theatre and ran the business affairs of the Frohman offices, and I, had tried to dissuade him. He laughed at us for our fear for him. This last letter of his read:

> The Metropolitan, Rochester, Minnesota, is scratched by this office, K. & E., and others. You did it and I am glad. As I telegraphed you I gave that play that I had intended for you a calm reading in my own home and I rather fear it is a bit old-fashioned and too talky. I have given it up. You see when one reads these things away from New York it is different and most anything is acceptable. It is different when you are at home. I know you like to be away from New York (I had written Frohman asking that the tour be ended). Alf Hayman has just told me how eager you are to continue after Los Angeles. If you play a week to cover the railroad fares it will be all right. Why a young man like you likes to continue on these tours I don't know. I hope to get away on May first and back shortly after you reach here. I am searching for something for you. Our last talk before you left for the West gave me much happiness.

When I received this letter I was days from New York, and there wasn't even time to write Frohman. I telegraphed and, after whatever private matters I had to tell him, I said:

> If you get yourself blown up by a submarine I'll never forgive you.

This was my last communication with the man who for twenty-three years had been my manager and with whom I had never had the slightest disagreement.

C. F. had a feeling, almost a superstitious feeling, that as I was his first star I must always be regarded and cherished and cosseted. William Gillette was his second star, but he had been a star before he came under Frohman's management.

I was in Vancouver when I heard that the "Lusitania" had been sunk, but we had no news of the people on the boat. We were on our way to our next stop, Everett, Washington; and there my acting manager and I sat up in the telegraph room of a small newspaper office for hours. Here we learned that Charles Frohman was among those lost.

CHAPTER THIRTY-TWO

S PEAK your piece good and you will get a big red
apple," was an ancient wheeze of the rural
schools.

When my niece, Ethel Barrymore, appeared for the
first time at the Garrick Theatre in New York in Clyde
Fitch's play, *Captain Jinks*, I gave her a large red
apple. This was the start of a custom that I have
since observed on the first night of the plays in which
not only my niece, but my two nephews, Lionel and
John Barrymore, appear. And in recent years my niece
and nephews have sent me a large red apple on the first
nights of the plays in which I have appeared.

The two Barrymore boys did not go on the stage so
early as their sister. They both thought of careers outside of the theatre, John as a newspaper artist and
Lionel as a painter. John was for a time on the art
staff of the *Evening Journal* in New York. He drew
clever but involved pictures. I remember one entitled
"The Web of Life," in which a lot of weird people
were trying to get across some place. It carried an
editorial note which began: "This is not an unpleas-
ant picture when looked at properly."

Shortly after 1900 they were all three on the stage, where practically every member of their family before them had been. John is the only one of the three Barrymores who has not played in my company. In May, 1914, my niece and I appeared at the Empire in Sardou's comedy, *A Scrap of Paper*, with this cast:

Prosper Couramont	John Drew
Baron De LaGlaciere	Charles Dalton
Brisemouche	Fuller Mellish
Anatole	Ernest Glendinning
Francois	Frank McCoy
Suzanne	Ethel Barrymore
Louise De LaGlaciere	Mary Boland
Mathilde	Charlotte Ives
Mlle. Zenobie	Jeffrys Lewis
Madame Dupont	Mrs. Thomas Whiffen
Pauline	Helen Collier

The season that I revived *Rosemary* I received from S. Yeghi, one of the Japanese commissioners to the Panama-Pacific International Exposition, a collection of eighteen character dolls, each one about half an inch high. They are all vividly colored and quaint, some grotesque and some serious. The letter that came with them was:

When I arrived at San Francisco I found that one very artistic friend sent me from Japan the

Photo. by Charlotte Fairchild.

John Drew.

dolls of eighteen plays of Kabuki. In Japan there has been for almost two hundred years the family of Ichikawa, the family of the best actors of Japan. In this family, if the son was not a good actor to represent the family, the best actor of the time was adopted to the family to bear the name of Ichikawa.

There are eighteen plays which were selected by this family, and they are called the Eighteen Plays of Kabuki. And to perform any of the eighteen plays, one should obtain permission of the family, even if he is an Ichikawa.

The dolls signify these eighteen plays of Kabuki. Kabuki could be translated as Drama, and in Kabuki there is also Dance included.

These dolls of Kabuki were first made about one hundred and fifty years ago, and they were not in fashion for the last fifty or sixty years. They are the remains of the art of the Tokugawa period and they are plain, simple dolls symbolizing the plays.

A friend of mine made these dolls for the first time in the last sixty years, and even in Japan they are very novel and interesting.

And it is my sincere wish to present these dolls to you, and I wish you would accept them with my sincere respect for your art. The dolls are entirely made with hand, they are modeled with hand and colored by hand.

Your *Rosemary* is the only "Remembrance" that would make me think of America when I return back to Japan. Particularly I could not forget that last scene of *Rosemary*, so impressively lonesome.

I could not forgive myself for not being able to see you in New York.

I am going back to Japan in about one month, after settling our affairs at the Exposition.

And I am greatly anxious to have two photographs of yourself, one in stage costume, and one in which you appear as yourself.

And before your photographs, I would tell the young people of Japan of your artful acting, for which I am certain they would pay you the best and highest respect.

Though this country has had no theatrical family which can boast, like the Ichikawa, of two hundred years in the theatre, there have been several families closely identified with the stage. In an editorial article called "Acting Blood," the *New York Herald* a few years ago printed:

> The theatrical profession has produced families in which the acting blood ran strong through more than one generation. The Booths, Jeffersons and Davenports were notable examples of inherited talent, and still more distinguished, in the eyes of the present generation of playgoers, are the Drews, now conspicuously in the public eye. The founder of the family was John Drew, one of the best Irish comedians our stage has known, who flourished during the fifties and whose wife, Mrs. John Drew, was a famous *Mrs. Malaprop.*

My daughter, Louise Drew, the granddaughter of two famous actresses of the American stage, my mother,

Louisa Drew, and Alexina Fisher Baker, and the great granddaughter of the English actress, Eliza Kinloch, together with the three children of my sister, Georgie Drew Barrymore, herself an actress of fine talent, are carrying on the family tradition and demonstrating the possession of "acting blood" in the fourth generation.

INDEX

A

Abbey, Edwin A, 106, 136.
Adams, Annie, 50, 171, 178.
Adams, Maude, 50, 169, 170, 171, 173, 177, 178, 183, 184, 186, 217.
After Business Hours, 109.
Aldrich, Thomas Bailey, 159, 161.
All the Comforts of Home, 170.
Allen, C. Leslie, 171, 177, 184.
Amberly, Lady, 11.
Amberly, Lord, 11.
American, The, 61.
Arabian Night, An, 78.
Archer, Fred, 147.
Arkansas Traveler, The, 37, 38.
Armstrong, Sydney, 182.
As You Like It, 95, 96, 98, 137, 140.
Ayling, Herbert, 184.

B

Baker, Alexina Fisher, 38, 233.
Baker, Josephine. *See* Mrs. John Drew.
Baker, Lewis, 38, 60, 61, 177, 184, 193, 199, 203.
Bancrofts, The, 146.
Barnes, Maggie, 76.
Barrett, Lawrence, 94, 96, 159, 161.
Barrett, Wilson, 93.
Barrie, J. M., 197, 218.
Barry, Nigel, 217.
Barrymore, Ethel, 56, 188, 190, 200, 218, 229, 230, 233.
Barrymore, John, 204, 229, 230, 233.
Barrymore, Lionel, 202, 203, 229, 230, 233.
Barrymore, Maurice, 54, 57, 58, 59, 62, 63, 64, 66, 67, 68, 69.

Barrymore, Mrs. Maurice. *See* Georgie Drew.
Bauble Shop, The, 183.
Beau Brummel, 171.
Beekman, W. H., 114.
Belasco, David, 182.
Bell, Constance, 204.
Bell, E. Hamilton, 93, 110, 112.
Belleville, Frederick de, 110.
Bells, The, 60.
Belmont, Anna, 184.
Benedict, E. C., 159.
Bennett, Frank V., 76, 77, 165, 166.
Berkeley, Marie, 217.
Bernhardt, Sarah, 61, 138, 199, 200.
Big Bonanza, The, 41, 43, 45, 46, 47, 48.
Bispham, William, 159, 161.
Blowitz, M. de, 142.
Boland, Mary, 197, 212, 213, 216, 217, 220, 230.
Bond, Frederick, 93, 101, 112, 114, 116.
Booth, Agnes, 98.
Booth, Edwin, 8, 24, 31, 54, 56, 57, 58, 91, 159, 160, 232.
Boots at the Swan, 88.
Bosworth, Hobart, 96, 98, 100, 116.
Bouchier, Arthur, 139.
Boucicault, Dion, 47, 86, 182.
Boughton, George, 137.
Bowers, Mrs. D. P., 8, 165, 183.
Bowkett, Sidney, 116.
Bradley, Malcolm, 217.
Brand, John, 84.
Brighton, 151.
Brough, Fannie, 203, 204.
Brown, Allston, 114.
Browning, Robert, 137.